JUNIOR CERTIFI

LESS STRESS
MORE
SUCCESS

Maths Revision
Ordinary Level
Paper 1

Brendan Guildea & Louise Boylan

Gill & Macmillan

Gill & Macmillan

Hume Avenue

Park West

Dublin 12

www.gillmacmillan.ie

978 07171 5958 1

Print origination and artwork by MPS Limited

The paper used in this book is made from the wood pulp of managed forests.

For every tree felled, at least one tree is planted, thereby renewing natural resources.

For permission to reproduce photographs, the authors and publisher gratefully acknowledge the following:

© Alamy: 43, 124, 140; © Photocall: 130; © Shutterstock: 59, 60, 61, 62, 76, 92, 95, 116L, 137, 158; © Shutterstock/Ingvar Bjork: 116R; © Shutterstock/titus manea: 161.

The authors and publisher have made every effort to trace all copyright holders, but if any has been inadvertently overlooked we would be pleased to make the necessary arrangement at the first opportunity.

Acknowledgements

The authors would like to thank Carol Guildea, Joe Heron and Jack Mahon who helped with the proofreading, checked the answers and made valuable suggestions that are included in the final text.

CONTENTS

Please note:
- The philosophy of Project Maths is that topics can overlap, so you may encounter Paper 1 material on Paper 2 and vice versa.
- The exam questions marked by the symbol in this book are selected from the following:
  1. SEC exam papers
  2. Sample exam papers
  3. Original and sourced exam-type questions

Introduction

aims
- ☐ To learn how to revise most effectively.
- ☐ To familiarise yourself with the structure of the exam paper.
- ☐ To learn to allocate the correct time for each question.
- ☐ To know and understand the words which appear often on the exam paper.
- ☐ To familiarise yourself with the syllabus.

The aim of this revision book is to help you get as high a mark as possible in your Junior Certificate. This book is designed to be exam focused. To do this, the book is based not just on the syllabus, but also on the examination paper. As a result, this revision book can be used in conjunction with **any** textbook.

Graded examples and exam questions

Throughout this book, **examples and exam questions are graded by level of difficulty**.

The level of difficulty is indicated by calculator symbols, as follows:

The number of calculators shown beside a question helps you know how difficult the question is. One calculator indicates a question which is relatively basic. As the questions get harder, the symbol will have more calculators. Three calculators will indicate an average-level question, whereas five calculators indicate that it is a very challenging question. These questions may be beyond some students, but give them a go! **Students hoping to achieve an A grade should aim to complete all of the 'five calculator' questions. The calculator symbol given for each question relates to the most difficult part of that question. Do not be discouraged by a challenging question.** In the Junior Certificate exam, difficult questions can sometimes begin with one or two simple parts; you should attempt as much as you can.

Preparing for your Junior Certificate Maths exam

It is very important to realise that **you are your own best teacher**. Revision is when you begin to teach yourself. Thus, it is very important for you to start your revision as soon as possible. Make notes while you are revising. If you are having difficulty with a particular question, seek help from your teacher, a friend or a member of your family. As with all subjects, the best examination preparation is to work through past examination or sample papers so that you are familiar with the layout and style of questions.

So let's start at the beginning. If you want to do well in your Junior Certificate, then two things are essential:

- Revise effectively.
- Be familiar with the exam paper and so be prepared on the day of the exam.

These may seem obvious, but it's worth taking a moment to think about what these tips mean.

How to revise most effectively

If you are going to do well in the Junior Certificate, you are going to spend quite a bit of time revising. Spending a little time learning how to revise effectively will help you get more from your time and help you absorb and understand more of the material on the course. Here are some tips to help you revise for maths.

- Find a quiet place where you can work. This place should be dedicated to study, free of potential distractions. Turn off all music, the TV, computer and mobile phone.
- Draw up a study plan. Don't be afraid to ask your parents/teachers/guidance counsellor for help at this stage.
- Do the more challenging revision first, when you are fresh. Trying to focus on difficult problems when you are tired can be counter-productive.
- Project Maths is based on understanding, so while you can 'learn' some elements of the course, it is important that you develop an understanding of the material.
- Drill and practice are essential ingredients for success in maths.
- Try to link any new material to things you know already. This is learning through association and helps long-term retention.

Study in small chunks lasting 25 to 35 minutes. Your memory and concentration will work better if you study in short bursts, but often.

Don't get hung up on more difficult material. Concentrate on understanding the fundamental concepts and being able to answer all of the straightforward questions. Then, with time, you can build up to the more challenging problems.

Junior Certificate examination

Exam focus is critical to exam success. It is important to prepare yourself for the challenge you will face. By learning about the structure of the exam, you will learn how to maximise your points, allocate your time effectively and how to manage the paper in a calm manner.

There is no set number of questions on this examination paper. You must answer **all** questions.

Read the exam paper right through at the start to determine which question is the easiest one to start with. Your mind may also be subconsciously processing some of the other problems.

Questions do not necessarily carry equal marks. To help you manage your time during this examination, a maximum time for each question is suggested on the exam paper. **Do not spend more than the suggested time on any question.**

If you remain within these times, you should have about 10 minutes left to review your work.

Start with your best question, then your next best and so on. This way, if you are short of time, at least your best questions will be done.

Attempt marks are valuable, so it is vital that you attempt all questions.

Leave **NO** blanks.

Further exam tips

- There is no such thing as rough work in Maths – all work is relevant. If the examiner doesn't know how you reached an answer, even a correct answer, then full marks will usually not be awarded. Thus, **show all your work**.
- It is a good idea to show each stage of a calculation when using a calculator (in case you press a wrong key). **Familiarise yourself with your calculator. Know your book of tables and formulae well and write down any formula that you use**.

Your calculator and book of tables are two extremely valuable resources to have in the exam. Make sure that you are very familiar with how your calculator works and that you know how to perform all functions on it. Also familiarise yourself with the book of tables so that you do not waste any time in the exam trying to find formulae.

- Attempt marks (partial credit) will be awarded for any step in the right direction. Therefore, **make an attempt at each part of the question**. Even if you do not get the correct answer, you can still pick up most of the marks on offer if you show how you worked it out. Also, **draw a diagram where possible**, because this can help you to see the solution.

- If you cannot finish part of a question, leave a space and come back to it later. **Never scribble out any work or use Tipp-Ex.** Put a single line through it so that the examiner can still read it. **Avoid using pencil** because the writing can be very faint and difficult to read.

- **Do not judge the length of your answer based on the size of the space provided.** Sometimes large spaces are provided for questions where only a short solution is required.

- If you run out of space in your answer booklet, **ask the supervisor for more paper**. Then clearly write the number of the exam question and the solution on the extra paper.

Glossary of some common phrases used on the examination paper

Write down, State
You can write down your answer without showing any work. However, if you want you can show some workings.

Calculate, Find, Show that, Determine, Prove
Obtain your answers by showing all relevant work. Marks are available for showing the steps leading to your final answer or conclusion.

Solve
Find the solution, or root, of an equation. The solution is the value of the variable that makes the left-hand side balance with the right-hand side.

Evaluate
Usually means to work out, or find, a numerical value by putting in numbers for letters.

Comment on
After studying the given information or your answers, give your opinion on their significance.

Plot
Indicate the position of points on a graph, usually on the x- and y-planes.

Construct
Draw an accurate diagram, usually labelled, using a pencil, ruler, set square, compass and protractor. Leave all constructions on your diagram.

Sketch
Make a rough diagram or graph, labelled if needed.

Hence

You *must* use the answer, or result, from the previous part of the question.

Hence or otherwise

It is recommended that you use the answer, or result, from the previous part of the question, but other methods are acceptable.

Give your answer in the form . . .

This means the examiner wants the final answer in a particular form, for example as a fraction, in surd form, in index notation, etc. Watch out for this, as you will lose marks if your answer is not in the correct form.

Syllabus checklist for Junior Certificate Ordinary Level Maths Paper 1 exam

The philosophy of Project Maths is that topics can overlap, so you may encounter Paper 1 material on Paper 2 and vice versa.

Throughout your course you will be asked to apply your knowledge and skills to solve problems in familiar and unfamiliar contexts. In problem-solving, you should use some of the following strategies:

- Trial and improvement
- Draw a diagram
- Look for a pattern
- Act it out
- Draw a table
- Simplify the problem
- Use an equation
- Work backwards
- Eliminate possibilities

The syllabus stresses that in all aspects of the Junior Certificate Maths course, students should be able to:

☐ Explore patterns and formulate conjectures.

☐ Explain findings.

☐ Justify conclusions.

☐ Communicate mathematics verbally and in written form.

☐ Apply your knowledge and skills to solve problems in familiar and unfamiliar contexts.

☐ Analyse information presented verbally and translate it into mathematical form.

☐ Devise, select and use appropriate mathematical models, formulae or techniques to process information and to draw relevant conclusions.

Number systems

- [ ] Understand the different types of numbers
    - ○ $\mathbb{N}$: the set of natural numbers $\{1, 2, 3, 4. \ldots\}$
    - ○ $\mathbb{Z}$: the set of integers, including 0
    - ○ $\mathbb{Q}$: the set of rational numbers
    - ○ $\mathbb{R}$: the set of real numbers
    - ○ $\mathbb{R}\backslash\mathbb{Q}$: the set of irrational numbers
- [ ] Understand the binary operations of addition, subtraction, multiplication and division and the relationships between these operations, beginning with whole numbers and integers.
- [ ] Explore some of the laws that govern these operations and use mathematical models to reinforce the algorithms they commonly use.
- [ ] Revisit these operations in the context of rational numbers and refine, revise and consolidate their ideas.
- [ ] Learn strategies for computation that can be applied to any numbers; implicit in such computational methods are generalisations about numerical relationships involving the operations being used.
- [ ] Articulate the generalisation that underlies your strategy, firstly in the vernacular and then in symbolic language.
- [ ] Problems set in context, using diagrams to solve the problems so you can appreciate how the mathematical concepts are related to real life.
- [ ] Algorithms used to solve problems involving fractional amounts.
- [ ] Investigate models such as decomposition, skip counting, arranging items in arrays and accumulating groups of equal size to make sense of the operations of addition, subtraction, multiplication and division in $\mathbb{N}$ where the answer is in $\mathbb{N}$, including the inverse operations.
- [ ] Investigate the properties of arithmetic: commutative, associative and distributive laws and the relationships between them.
- [ ] Appreciate the order of operations, including the use of brackets.
- [ ] Investigate models such as the number line to illustrate the operations of addition, subtraction, multiplication and division in $\mathbb{Z}$.
- [ ] Generalise and articulate observations of arithmetic operations.
- [ ] Investigate models to help think about the operations of addition, subtraction, multiplication and division of rational numbers.
- [ ] Consolidate the idea that equality is a relationship in which two mathematical expressions hold the same value.
- [ ] Analyse solution strategies to problems.
- [ ] Engage with the idea of mathematical proof.
- [ ] Calculate percentages.

- ☐ Use the equivalence of fractions, decimals and percentages to compare proportions.
- ☐ Consolidate your understanding and your learning of factors, multiples and prime numbers in $\mathbb{N}$.
- ☐ Consolidate your understanding of the relationship between ratio and proportion.
- ☐ Check a result by considering whether it is of the right order of magnitude.
- ☐ Check a result by working the problem backwards.
- ☐ Justify approximations and estimates of calculations.
- ☐ Present numerical answers to degree of accuracy specified.

Expressions

- ☐ Use letters to represent quantities that are variable.
- ☐ Be able to perform arithmetic operations on expressions.
- ☐ Understand applications to real-life contexts.
- ☐ Understand transformational activities: collecting like terms, simplifying expressions, substituting, expanding and factoring.
- ☐ Evaluate expressions of the form
  - ○ $ax + by$
  - ○ $a(x + y)$
  - ○ axy
  - ○ $\dfrac{ax + by}{cx + dy}$
  - ○ $x^2 + bx + c$, where $a, b, c, d, x, y \in \mathbb{Z}$
- ☐ Add and subtract simple algebraic expressions of forms such as:
  - ○ $\dfrac{ax + b}{c} \pm \dfrac{dx + e}{f}$
  - ○ $(ax + by + c) \pm (dx + ey + f)$
  - ○ $(ax^2 + bx + c) \pm (dx^2 + ex + f)$, where $a, b, c, d, e, f \in \mathbb{Z}$
- ☐ Use the associative and distributive property to simplify such expressions as:
  - ○ $a(bx + cy + d) + e(fx + gy + h)$
  - ○ $a(bx^2 + cx + d)$
  - ○ $ax(bx^2 + c)$, where $a, b, c, d, e, f, g, h \in \mathbb{Z}$
- ☐ Multiply expressions of the form $(ax + b)(cx + d)$, where $a, b, c, d \in \mathbb{Z}$.
- ☐ Divide expressions of the form $ax^2 + bx + c \div dx + e$, where $a, b, c, d, e \in \mathbb{Z}$.

☐ Factorise expressions such as

- ○ ax, axy, where $a \in \mathbb{Z}$
- ○ $abxy + ay$, where $a, b \in \mathbb{Z}$
- ○ $sx - ty + tx - sy$, where s, t, x, y are variable
- ○ $ax^2 + bx$, where $a, b, c \in \mathbb{Z}$
- ○ $x^2 + bx + c$, where $b, c \in \mathbb{Z}$
- ○ $x^2 - a^2$

Equations and inequalities

☐ Use a variety of problem-solving strategies to solve equations and inequalities.

☐ Identify the necessary information and represent problems mathematically, making correct use of symbols, words, diagrams, tables and graphs.

☐ Consolidate your understanding of the concept of equality.

☐ Solve first-degree equations in one or two variables with coefficients elements of $\mathbb{Z}$ and solutions also in $\mathbb{Z}$.

☐ Solve quadratic equations of the form $x^2 + bx + c = 0$, where $b, c \in \mathbb{Z}$, and $x^2 + bx + c$ is factorisable.

☐ Solve simple problems leading to quadratic equations.

☐ Solve equations of the form $\dfrac{ax + b}{c} \pm \dfrac{dx + e}{f} = \dfrac{g}{h}$, where $a, b, c, d, e, f, g, h \in \mathbb{Z}$.

☐ Solve linear inequalities in one variable of the form $g(x) \leq k$, where $g(x) = ax + b$, $a \in \mathbb{N}$ and $b, k \in \mathbb{Z}$.

Indices

☐ Understand binary operations of addition, subtraction, multiplication and division in the context of numbers in index form.

☐ Use and apply some of the rules for indices.

☐ Use the notation $a^{\frac{1}{2}}$, $a \in \mathbb{N}$.

☐ Compute reciprocals.

Sets

☐ Learn set language as an international symbolic mathematical tool.

☐ Understand the concept of a set as being a well-defined collection of objects or elements.

☐ Understand the concept of the universal set, null set, subset, cardinal number; the union, intersection, set difference operators, and Venn diagrams.

☐ Investigate the properties of arithmetic as related to sets and solve problems involving sets.

☐ Use suitable set notation and terminology.

☐ List elements of a finite set.

☐ Describe the rule that defines a set.

☐ Consolidate the idea that equality of sets is a relationship in which two equal sets have the same elements.

☐ Perform the operations of:

  ○ Intersection

  ○ Union (for two sets)

  ○ Set difference

  ○ Complement

☐ Investigate the commutative property for intersection, union and difference.

Generating arithmetic expressions from repeating patterns

☐ Understand patterns and the rules that govern them.

☐ Understand a relationship as that which involves a set of inputs, a set of outputs and a correspondence from each input to each output.

☐ Use tables to represent a repeating-pattern situation.

☐ Generalise and explain patterns and relationships in words and numbers.

☐ Write arithmetic expressions for particular terms in a sequence.

Representing situations with tables, diagrams and graphs

☐ Understand relations derived from some kind of context — familiar, everyday situations, imaginary contexts or arrangements of tiles or blocks.

☐ Look at various patterns and make predictions about what comes next.

☐ Use tables, diagrams and graphs as tools for representing and analysing linear, quadratic and exponential patterns and relations (exponential relations limited to doubling and tripling).

☐ Develop and use your own generalising strategies and ideas and consider those of others.

☐ Present and interpret solutions, explaining and justifying methods, inferences and reasoning.

Finding formulae

☐ Find ways to express a general relationship arising from a pattern or context.

☐ Find the underlying formula written in words from which the data is derived (linear relations).

Examining algebraic relationships

☐ Understand features of a relationship and how these features appear in the different representations.

☐ Understand constant rate of change: linear relationships.

☐ Understand non-constant rate of change: quadratic relationships.

☐ Understand proportional relationships.

☐ Show that relations have features that can be represented in a variety of ways.

☐ Distinguish those features that are especially useful to identify and point out how those features appear in different representations: in tables, graphs, physical models and formulas expressed in words and algebraically.

☐ Use the representations to reason about the situation from which the relationship is derived and communicate your thinking to others.

☐ Recognise that a distinguishing feature of quadratic relations is the way change varies.

☐ Discuss rate of change and the y-intercept, consider how these relate to the context from which the relationship is derived, and identify how they can appear in a table, in a graph and in a formula.

☐ Decide if two linear relations have a common value (decide if two lines intersect and where the intersection occurs).

☐ Investigate relations of the form $y = mx$ and $y = mx + c$.

☐ Recognise problems involving direct proportion and identify the necessary information to solve them.

Relations without formulae

☐ Use graphs to represent phenomena quantitatively.

☐ Explore graphs of motion.

☐ Make sense of quantitative graphs and draw conclusions from them.

☐ Make connections between the shape of a graph and the story of a phenomenon.

☐ Describe both quantity and change of quantity on a graph.

Applied measure

☐ Calculate, interpret and apply units of measure and time.

☐ Solve problems that involve calculating average speed, distance and time.

Functions

☐ Understand the meaning and notation associated with functions.

☐ Engage with the concept of a function, domain, co-domain and range.

☐ Make use of function notation $f(x) =$, $f: x \rightarrow$, and $y =$.

Graphing functions

☐ Be able to interpret and represent linear, quadratic and exponential functions in graphical form.

☐ Interpret simple graphs.

☐ Plot points and lines.

☐ Draw graphs of the following functions and interpret equations of the form $f(x) = g(x)$ as a comparison of functions:
  ○ $f(x) = ax$, where $a \in \mathbb{Z}$
  ○ $f(x) = ax + b$, where $a, b \in \mathbb{Z}$
  ○ $f(x) = ax^2 + bx + c$, where $a \in \mathbb{N}, b, c \in \mathbb{Z}, x \in \mathbb{R}$

☐ Use graphical methods to find approximate solutions where $f(x) = g(x)$ and interpret the results.

☐ Graph solution sets on the number line for linear inequalities in one variable.

Applied arithmetic

☐ Make value for money calculations and judgments.

☐ Use ratio and proportionality.

☐ Solve problems that involve:
  ○ Mobile phone tariffs
  ○ Currency transactions
  ○ Shopping
  ○ VAT
  ○ Meter readings
  ○ Cost price
  ○ Selling price
  ○ Loss and percentage loss
  ○ Profit and percentage profit
  ○ Discount and percentage discount
  ○ Compound interest (not more than 3 years)
  ○ Income tax (standard rate only)
  ○ Net pay (including other deductions)

aims

- [ ] To learn what the symbols ℕ, ℤ, ℚ, and ℝ represent
- [ ] To be familiar with prime numbers, factors and the fundamental theorem of arithmetic
- [ ] To be able to find LCM and HCF as required

Natural numbers ℕ

The positive whole numbers 1, 2, 3, 4, 5, 6, . . . are also called the counting numbers. The dots indicate that the numbers go on forever and have no end (infinite).

exam Q

Give two reasons why −7·3 is not a natural number.

Solution

Reason 1. It is a negative number

Reason 2. It is not a whole number (it is a decimal)

Factors (divisors)

key point

The factors of any whole number are the whole numbers that divide exactly into the given number, leaving no remainder.

1 is a factor of every number.

Every number is a factor of itself.

Example

Find the highest common factor of 18 and 45.

Solution

18		45	
1 × 18		1 × 45	
2 × 9		3 × 15	
3 × 6		5 × 9	

The common factors are 1, 3 and 9.

The highest common factor of 18 and 45 is 9.

key point

The highest common factor of two or more numbers is the largest factor that is common to each of the given numbers.

Example

In these productogons, the number in each square is the product of the numbers in the circles on each side of it. Find the missing numbers in each of these productogons.

Solution

key point

The use of the word productogon in the question indicates we use multiplication. This is because product means multiply.

(i)

(ii)

Prime numbers

A prime number is a whole number greater than 1 that has only two factors, 1 and itself.

The first 12 prime numbers are

2, 3, 5, 7, 11, 13, 17, 19, 23, 29, 31 and 37.

There is an infinite number of prime numbers.

Numbers that have more than two factors are called composite numbers, e.g. 20 has 1, 2, 4, 5, 10, 20 as factors.

The fundamental theorem of arithmetic states that any whole number greater than 1 can be written as the product of its prime factors in a **unique** way. This will underpin many exam questions on number theory.

Prime factors

Any number can be expressed as a product of prime numbers. To express the number 180 as a product of its prime numbers, first divide by the smallest prime number that will divide exactly into it.

The smallest prime number 2 : $2\,|\,180$
The smallest prime 2 again   : $2\,|\,\overline{90}$
The smallest prime 3   : $3\,|\,\overline{45}$
The smallest prime 3 again   : $3\,|\,\overline{15}$
The smallest prime 5   : $5\,|\,\overline{5}$
                                $\overline{1}$

So 180 expressed as a product of primes is:

$$2 \times 2 \times 3 \times 3 \times 5 = 2^2 \times 3^2 \times 5$$

Example 1

For security, a credit card is encrypted using prime factors. A huge number is assigned to each individual card and it can only be verified by its prime factor decomposition. Find the 10-digit natural number which is assigned to the following credit cards whose prime factor decomposition is

(i) $2^2 \times 11 \times 13 \times 17^2 \times 19^3$
(ii) $2^7 \times 3^2 \times 5^2 \times 7^3 \times 23 \times 31$

Solution

By calculator: (i) 1133847572
                 (ii) 7043299200

Example 2

Gepetto makes wooden puppets. He has three lengths of wood which he wants to cut into pieces, all of which must be the same length and be as long as possible. The lengths of the three pieces of wood are 315cm, 357cm and 252cm.

(i) Express each of the three lengths as a product of primes.
(ii) Hence, calculate what length each piece should be and how many pieces he will have.

Solution

(i)

```
3 | 315
3 | 105
5 |  35
7 |   7
  |   1
```

```
 3 | 357
 7 | 119
17 |  17
   |   1
```

```
2 | 252
2 | 126
3 |  63
3 |  21
7 |   7
  |   1
```

$$3^2 \times 5 \times 7 \qquad 3 \times 7 \times 17 \qquad 2^2 \times 3^2 \times 7$$

(ii) By observation of the three product of primes above, the highest common factor (HCF) is given by $3 \times 7 = 21$.

Hence, each piece of wood should be 21cm long.

key point

3×7 is common to all three lengths.

The number of pieces is given

by $\dfrac{315}{21} + \dfrac{357}{21} + \dfrac{252}{21}$

$= 15 + 17 + 12$

$= 44$

Multiples and the lowest common multiple (LCM)

> The multiples of a number are found by multiplying the number by 1, 2, 3 . . . and so on.

The multiples of 4 are: 4, 8, 12, 16, 20...............

The multiples of 7 are: 7, 14, 21, 28, 35.............

> The **lowest common multiple** of two or more numbers is the **smallest multiple** that is common to each of the numbers.

In other words, the lowest common multiple is the **smallest** number into which each of the numbers will divide exactly.

For example, the lowest common multiple of 2, 4 and 7 is 28, as 28 is the smallest number into which 2, 4 and 7 will all divide exactly.

The lowest common multiple of two or more numbers is found with the following steps:

1. Write down the multiples of each number.
2. The lowest common multiple is the smallest (first) multiple they have in common.

Example

K is the set of natural numbers from 1 to 25, inclusive.

(i) List the elements of K that are multiples of 3.

(ii) List the elements of K that are multiples of 5.

(iii) Write down the lowest common multiple of 3 and 5.

Solution

K = {1, 2, 3, 4, 5, 6, 7, 8, 9, 10, 11, 12, 13, 14, 15, 16, 17, 18, 19, 20, 21, 22, 23, 24, 25}

(i) Multiples of 3 = {3, 6, 9, 12, 15, 18, 21, 24}

(ii) Multiples of 5 = {5, 10, 15, 20, 25}

(iii) Lowest common multiple (LCM) is 15.

   That is the smallest number that both sets have in common.

Integers $\mathbb{Z}$

Negative numbers are numbers below zero. Positive and negative **whole** numbers, including zero, are called integers.

Integers can be represented on a number line:

Integers to the right of zero are called **positive integers**.

Integers to the left of zero are called **negative integers**.

Example

At midnight on Christmas Eve the temperatures in some cities were as shown in the table.

(i) Which city recorded the

    (a) Lowest temperature

    (b) Highest temperature?

(ii) List the temperatures from coldest to hottest.

(iii) Which cities had a temperature difference of 6°C?

(iv) What is the difference in temperature between

    (a) Dublin and Moscow

    (b) Cairo and Dublin?

New York	2°C
Rome	−2°C
Dublin	−1°C
Moscow	−20°C
Cairo	4°C

Solution

(i) (a) Lowest temperature, $-20°$, in Moscow.

    (b) Highest temperature, $4°$, in Cairo.

(ii) $-20, -2, -1, 2, 4$

(iii)

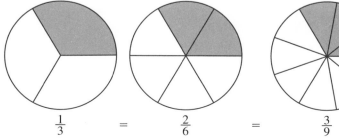 Rome and Cairo have a difference of 6°C

(iv) (a) Dublin and Moscow $= -1 - (-20) = -1 + 20 = 19°$

    (b) Cairo and Dublin $= 4 - (-1) = 4 + 1 = 5°$

Fractions (rational numbers)

A fraction is written as two whole numbers, one over the other, separated by a bar. Equivalent fractions are fractions that are equal.

For example:

$$\frac{1}{3} = \frac{2}{6} = \frac{3}{9} = \frac{4}{12}$$

This can be shown on a diagram where the same proportion is shaded in each circle.

key point

$$\text{Fraction} = \frac{\text{Numerator}}{\text{Denominator}}$$

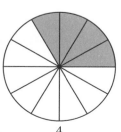

$$\frac{1}{3} \quad = \quad \frac{2}{6} \quad = \quad \frac{3}{9} \quad = \quad \frac{4}{12}$$

A rational number (fraction) is a number that can be written as a ratio, $\frac{p}{q}$, of two integers, p and q, but $q \neq 0$.

Examples are $\dfrac{7}{2}$, $-\dfrac{11}{19}$, $8 = \dfrac{8}{1}$, $0 = \dfrac{0}{1}$, $5 \cdot 23 = \dfrac{523}{100}$

Rational numbers are denoted by the letter $\mathbb{Q}$.

Example

Bren is trying to subtract $\frac{1}{5}$ from $\frac{7}{8}$.

His attempt is shown here: $\frac{7}{8} - \frac{1}{5} = \frac{6}{3} = 2$.

(i) Explain what Bren has done wrong.

(ii) Write out the correct solution.

Solution

(i) It seems that Bren has subtracted the top numbers and subtracted the bottom numbers.

For subtraction or addition of fractions, we must find a common denominator.

(ii) $\frac{7}{8} - \frac{1}{5} \Rightarrow$ common denominator $= 8 \times 5 = 40$

Then $\dfrac{7}{8} - \dfrac{1}{5} = \dfrac{(5)(7) - (8)(1)}{40} = \dfrac{35 - 8}{40} = \dfrac{27}{40}$.

See the chapter on algebraic expressions for more on addition/subtraction of fractions.

Sheila orders two pizzas to divide evenly between herself and five friends.

(i) What fraction of a pizza will each person get? Write your fraction in its simplest form.

(ii) One of the friends gets a text and leaves before the pizza is delivered. What fraction will each person now get if the pizzas are divided evenly between those remaining?

(iii) Find how much extra pizza each person gets.

Solution

(i) 2 pizzas $\div$ 6 $= \dfrac{2}{6} = \dfrac{1}{3}$ each

(ii) 2 pizzas $\div$ 5 $= \dfrac{2}{5}$ each

(iii) Extra pizza $= \dfrac{2}{5} - \dfrac{1}{3}$

$= \dfrac{(2)(3) - (1)(5)}{15}$ (common denominator $= 5 \times 3 = 15$)

$= \dfrac{6 - 5}{15}$

$= \dfrac{1}{15}$

exam Q

Three students completed a test but got their results in different ways. The teacher told Karen that she got 0·7 of the questions correct. John was told he got 80% of the questions correct. David was told he got $\frac{3}{4}$ of the questions correct.

(i) Which student got the best result? Give a reason for your answer.

(ii) There were 20 questions on the test. How many questions each did Karen, John and David answer correctly?

(iii) Find the mean number of correct answers.

Solution

(i) Karen got $0·7 = \frac{7}{10} = \frac{7 \times 100}{10}\% = 70\%$

John got 80%

David got $\frac{3}{4} = \frac{3 \times 100}{4}\% = 75\%$

By observation from the above work, John got the best result.

(ii) Karen got 70% of $20 = \frac{70}{100} \times 20 = 14$ correct

John got 80% of $20 = \frac{80}{100} \times 20 = 16$ correct

David got 75% of $20 = \frac{75}{100} \times 20 = 15$ correct

(iii) Mean $= \frac{14 + 16 + 15}{3} = \frac{45}{3} = 15$

 exam focus

The question was awarded 20 marks in total, as follows.

Part i 10 marks, with 5 marks awarded for one correct piece of work.

Part ii 5 marks, with 3 marks awarded for one correct piece of work.

Part iii 5 marks, with 3 marks awarded for one correct piece of work.

Hence, with 11 marks out of 20 marks awarded for no correct answers, you can see the importance of attempting every part of every question.

(i) (a) In the diagram below, what fraction of row **A** is shaded?

```
        R    S    T    U
   A  ┌────┬────┬────┬────┐
      │    │    │    │    │
   B  ├────┼────┼────┼────┤
      │    │    │    │    │
   C  ├────┼────┼────┼────┤
      │    │    │    │    │
   D  ├────┼────┼────┼────┤
      │    │    │    │    │
   E  ├────┼────┼────┼────┤
      │    │    │    │    │
   F  ├────┼────┼────┼────┤
      │    │    │    │    │
   G  └────┴────┴────┴────┘
```

(b) In the same diagram, what fraction of column **R** is shaded?

(c) Using the diagram or otherwise, calculate the result when your fractions in part **(a)** and part **(b)** are multiplied.

(ii) Tim claims that the two fractions shown by the shading of the strips **X** and **Y** below are the same. Is Tim correct? Give a reason for your answer.

```
┌─────┬─────┬─────┬─────┬─────┐
│     │     │     │     │     │  X
└─────┴─────┴─────┴─────┴─────┘
```

```
┌───────┬───────┬───────┐
│       │       │       │  Y
└───────┴───────┴───────┘
```

Solution

(i) (a) Count the shaded boxes in row A = 3

Answer $\dfrac{3}{4}$

(b) Count the shaded boxes in column R = 5

Answer $\dfrac{5}{7}$

(c) Method 1 $\dfrac{3}{4} \times \dfrac{5}{7} = \dfrac{15}{28}$

Method 2   Count all the shaded boxes in the diagram = 15

Count every box in the diagram = 28

Answer $\dfrac{15}{28}$

(ii) Strip X has 3 boxes shaded out of 5 $= \dfrac{3}{5}$

Strip Y has 2 boxes shaded out of 3 $= \dfrac{2}{3}$

Since $\dfrac{3}{5} \neq \dfrac{2}{3}$, Tim is not correct.

(i) Write $\dfrac{3}{8}$ as a decimal.

(ii) Represent the numbers $\frac{3}{8}$ and 0·4 on the number line below.

0   1

(iii) How could the number line in **(ii)** above help you decide which is the bigger of the two numbers?

Solution

(i) $\dfrac{3}{8} = 0{\cdot}375$

(ii)

0·4

0   0·375   1

(iii) The number to the right-hand side on a number line is always the bigger of the two numbers.

0·4 is the bigger number.

Real numbers

The natural numbers ($\mathbb{N}$) are a subset of the integers ($\mathbb{Z}$).

The integers ($\mathbb{Z}$) are a subset of the rational numbers ($\mathbb{Q}$).

The rational numbers ($\mathbb{Q}$) are a subset of the real numbers ($\mathbb{R}$).

The number sets are in the formulae and tables booklet, which is available to you in the examination.

The following Venn diagram summarises the number system.

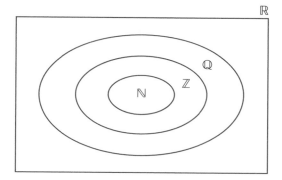

See the chapter on sets, where the first exam question illustrates the way the examiner links sets and the number system.

The numbers outside the set $\mathbb{Q}$ are called irrational numbers. You will study irrational numbers at Leaving Certificate.

The columns in the table below represent the following sets of numbers: natural numbers ($\mathbb{N}$), integers ($\mathbb{Z}$), rational numbers ($\mathbb{Q}$). Complete the table by writing either YES or NO into each box, indicating whether each of the numbers -23, $\frac{1}{2}$, 7^2, $2\cdot95$, 0, 47 is or is not an element of each.

(One box has already been filled in. The YES indicates that the number 47 is an element of the set of rational numbers, $\mathbb{Q}$.)

Set \ Number	-23	$\frac{1}{2}$	7^2	$2\cdot95$	0	47
$\mathbb{N}$						
$\mathbb{Z}$						
$\mathbb{Q}$						Yes

Solution

$7^2 = 49$ and 47 are the only natural numbers, $\mathbb{N}$, in the question. 49, 47, 0 and -23 are the only integers, $\mathbb{Z}$, and all six numbers are rational, $\mathbb{Q}$.

Set \ Number	-23	$\frac{1}{2}$	7^2	$2\cdot95$	0	47
$\mathbb{N}$	No	No	Yes	No	No	Yes
$\mathbb{Z}$	Yes	No	Yes	No	Yes	Yes
$\mathbb{Q}$	Yes	Yes	Yes	Yes	Yes	Yes

2 Algebraic Expressions

aims
□ To learn how to evaluate expressions.
□ To learn how to simplify algebraic expressions.
□ To learn how to add and subtract algebraic fractions.

Evaluating expressions

To evaluate expressions given the value of the variables, substitute the values in for the variables and evaluate the expression. When replacing a letter with a number, it is **good practice to put the number in a bracket**.

Example

Find the value of $4x + 5$ when $x = 3$.

Solution

$4x + 5$

$4(3) + 5$ (let $x = 3$)

$12 + 5$

17

key point

Once you have substituted in the given values, you can use your calculator to simplify the calculations required.

Example

Find the value of $2a^2 - 11$ when $a = 4$.

Solution

$2a^2 - 11$

$2(4)^2 - 11$ (let $a = 4$)

$2(16) - 11$

$32 - 11$

21

exam focus

Evaluating expressions is a vital skill for you to have throughout all aspects of your maths course.

Example

If $p = -4$, find the value of:

(i) $3p + 5$

(ii) $2p^2 - 5$

key point

Take care when substituting in negative values. Always put brackets around these, then simplify the expression.

Solution

(i) $3p + 5$

$\quad 3(-4) + 5$

$\quad -12 + 5$

$\quad -7$

(ii) $2p^2 - 5$

$\quad 2(-4)^2 - 5$

$\quad 2(16) - 5$

$\quad 32 - 5$

$\quad 27$

Given that $y = \sqrt{2x - a}$,

find the value of y when $x = 4$ and $a = -1$.

Solution

$y = \sqrt{2x - a}$

$y = \sqrt{2(4) - (-1)}$

$y = \sqrt{8 + 1}$

$y = \sqrt{9}$

$y = 3$

Find the values of the following expressions if $x = 3$ and $y = 5$.

(i) $5x + 4y$

(ii) $x^2 + y^2$

Solution

(i) $5x + 4y$ (let $x = 3$ and $y = 5$)

$\quad 5(3) + 4(5)$

$\quad 15 + 20$

$\quad 35$

(ii) $x^2 + y^2$ (let $x = 3$ and $y = 5$)

$\quad (3)^2 + (5)^2$

$\quad 9 + 25$

$\quad 34$

Find the values of the following expressions if $a = 4$ and $b = -1$.

(i) $2a + 3b - 2$

(ii) $a^2 + b^2 + 4$

(iii) $\dfrac{a + 2b}{2}$

Solution

$a = 4$ and $b = -1$ in each case:

(i) $2a + 3b - 2$

$2(4) + 3(-1) - 2$

$8 - 3 - 2$

3

(ii) $a^2 + b^2 + 4$

$(4)^2 + (-1)^2 + 4$

$16 + 1 + 4$

21

(iii) $\dfrac{a + 2b}{2}$

$\dfrac{4 + 2(-1)}{2}$

$\dfrac{4 - 2}{2}$

$\dfrac{2}{2}$

1

Simplifying algebraic expressions

You must be able to apply the associative and distributive properties when simplifying algebraic expressions.

Associative property	Distributive property
$(A \times B) \times C = A \times (B \times C)$	$A(B + C) = AB + AC$
	$(A + B)(C + D) = A(C + D) + B(C + D)$

Example

Simplify $5(4x - 2) - 7(2x - 5)$.

Solution

$5(4x - 2) - 7(2x - 5)$ (remember, $-7 \times -5 = 35$)

$20x - 10 - 14x + 35$ (multiply out the brackets)

$6x + 25$ (add like terms)

key point

Add and subtract like terms.

Example

Write in its simplest form: $(3x + 2y) - 2(x + 3y - 4)$.

Solution

$(3x + 2y) - 2(x + 3y - 4)$

$3x + 2y - 2x - 6y + 8$

$x - 4y + 8$

Example

Simplify $2a(4a + 3) - 4(3a - 7)$.

Solution

$2a(4a + 3) - 4(3a - 7)$

$8a^2 + 6a - 12a + 28$ (multiply out the brackets)

$8a^2 - 6a + 28$ (add like terms)

(i) Multiply $5(3a - 4b)$.

(ii) Multiply $x(x - y) + y(x + y)$. Write the answer in its simplest form.

Solution

(i) $5(3a - 4b)$

    $15a - 20b$

(ii) $x(x - y) + y(x + y)$

            $x^2 - xy + xy + y^2$

            $x^2 + y^2$

The entire question was worth 5 marks.

4 marks were awarded for getting either **(i)** or **(ii)** correct.

3 marks were awarded having any correct multiplication.

Example

Simplify $(x + 3)(x - 4)$.

Solution

Method 1: Use the distributive law

$(x + 3)(x - 4)$

$x(x - 4) + 3(x - 4)$ (remember, $+3 \times -4 = -12$)

$x^2 - 4x + 3x - 12$ (multiply out the brackets)

$x^2 - x - 12$ (add like terms)

> **key point**
>
> There are two methods for multiplying out brackets. These are both shown in this example. You can use whichever method you prefer.

Method 2: Use the box method

Put the terms in the first bracket on the top and terms from the second bracket down the side. Multiply each term by each other term.

	x	$+3$
x	x^2	$+3x$
-4	$-4x$	-12

Listing all terms from inside the boxes:

$x^2 - 4x + 3x - 12$

$x^2 - x - 12$ (add like terms)

Multiply $(3x - 2)$ by $(4x + 5)$ and write your answer in its simplest form.

Solution

Using the box method:

	$3x$	-2
$4x$	$12x^2$	$-8x$
5	$15x$	-10

$= 12x^2 + 15x - 8x - 10$

$= 12x^2 + 7x - 10$

> **key point**
>
> You can use either the distributive law **or** the box method to multiply out expressions. Use whichever method you are most comfortable with.

Example

Simplify $(3p + 2q)(p - 3q)$.

Solution

$(3p + 2q)(p - 3q)$

$3p(p - 3q) + 2q(p - 3q)$ (using the distributive law)

$3p^2 - 9pq + 2pq - 6q^2$ (multiply out the brackets)

$3p^2 - 7pq - 6q^2$ (add like terms)

Example

Simplify $(5a - 7)^2$.

Solution

$(5a - 7)^2 = (5a - 7)(5a - 7)$

key point

A common mistake here is for candidates to just square the first term and square the second term, getting $25a^2 + 49$. This is incorrect. You **must** multiply out as shown.

	$5a$	-7
$5a$	$25a^2$	$-35a$
-7	$-35a$	$+49$

$25a^2 - 35a - 35a + 49$ (using the box method)

$25a^2 - 70a + 49$ (add like terms)

exam Q

Multiply $(x - 2)$ by $(3x + 11)$ and hence evaluate your answer when $x = -2$.

Solution

Using the distributive law:

$(x - 2)(3x + 11)$

$x(3x + 11) - 2(3x + 11)$

$3x^2 + 11x - 6x - 22$ (multiply out the brackets)

$3x^2 + 5x - 22$ (add like terms)

exam focus

The word 'hence' means that you **must** simplify the expression first and **then** let $x = -2$.

Evaluate $3x^2 + 5x - 22$ when $x = -2$: $3(-2)^2 + 5(-2) - 22$

$3(4) - 10 - 22$

$12 - 32$

-20

Adding and subtracting algebraic fractions

Algebraic fractions that have numbers as denominators can be added or subtracted in exactly the same way as in arithmetic, i.e. we express the fractions with the lowest common denominator (the LCM of the denominators). Adding fractions was covered in the chapter on number systems.

Algebraic fractions are added or subtracted with the following steps:

1. Put brackets in where necessary.
2. Find the LCM of the expressions on the bottom.
3. Proceed in exactly the same way as in arithmetic.
4. Simplify the top (add and subtract terms which are the same).

Study the next example to understand the steps involved in adding and subtracting algebraic fractions.

Example

Write as a simple fraction: $\dfrac{x}{3} + \dfrac{5x}{6}$.

Solution

$$\frac{x}{3} + \frac{5x}{6}$$

$$\frac{?(x) + ?(5x)}{6}$$ (the LCM of the denominators is 6)

$$\frac{2(x) + ?(5x)}{6}$$ (3 divides into 6 two times.
Multiply 2 by the term on top of the 3.)

$$\frac{2(x) + 1(5x)}{6}$$ (6 divides into 6 one time.
Multiply 1 by the term on top of the 6.)

$$\frac{2x + 5x}{6}$$ (multiply out the brackets)

$$\frac{7x}{6}$$ (simplify)

Example

Express $\dfrac{x+7}{3} - \dfrac{x}{9}$ as a single fraction.

Give your answer in its simplest form.

Solution

$\dfrac{(x+7)}{3} - \dfrac{(x)}{9}$ (put brackets on top)

$\dfrac{?(x+7) - ?(x)}{9}$ (LCM of the denominators 3 and 9 is 9)

$\dfrac{3(x+7) - ?(x)}{9}$ (3 divides into 9 three times. Multiply 3 by the term on top of the 3.)

$\dfrac{3(x+7) - 1(x)}{9}$ (9 divides into 9 one time. Multiply 1 by the term on top of the 9.)

$\dfrac{3x + 21 - x}{9}$ (multiply out the brackets)

$\dfrac{2x + 21}{9}$ (simplify the top)

Express $\dfrac{x+3}{2} + \dfrac{2x-1}{5}$ as a single fraction.

Solution

$\dfrac{(x+3)}{2} + \dfrac{(2x-1)}{5}$ (put brackets on top)

$\dfrac{?(x+3) + ?(2x-1)}{10}$ (LCM of the denominators 2 and 5 is 10)

$\dfrac{5(x+3) + ?(2x-1)}{10}$ (2 divides into 10 five times. Multiply 5 by the term on top of the 2.)

$\dfrac{5(x+3) + 2(2x-1)}{10}$ (5 divides into 10 two times. Multiply 2 by the term on top of the 5.)

$\dfrac{5x + 15 + 4x - 2}{10}$ (multiply out the brackets)

$\dfrac{9x + 13}{10}$ (simplify the top)

(i) Express $\dfrac{3x + 2}{4} - \dfrac{x + 4}{5}$ as a single fraction.

Give your answer in its simplest form.

(ii) Verify your answer to part **(i)** by letting $x = 6$.

Solution

(i) $\dfrac{(3x + 2)}{4} - \dfrac{(x + 4)}{5}$ (put brackets on top)

$\dfrac{?(3x + 2) - ?(x + 4)}{20}$ (LCM of the denominators 4 and 5 is 20)

$\dfrac{5(3x + 2) - ?(x + 4)}{20}$ (4 divides into 20 five times. Multiply 5 by the term on top of the 4.)

$\dfrac{5(3x + 2) - 4(x + 4)}{20}$ (5 divides into 20 four times. Multiply 4 by the term on top of the 5.)

$\dfrac{15x + 10 - 4x - 16}{20}$ (multiply out the brackets)

$\dfrac{11x - 6}{20}$ (multiply out the brackets)

(ii) Let $x = 6$ in the original fractions:

$\dfrac{3x + 2}{4} - \dfrac{x + 4}{5}$

$\dfrac{3(6) + 2}{4} - \dfrac{(6) + 4}{5}$

$\dfrac{18 + 2}{4} - \dfrac{6 + 4}{5}$

$\dfrac{20}{4} - \dfrac{10}{5}$

$5 - 2$

3

Let $x = 6$ in the single fraction:

$\dfrac{11x - 6}{20}$

$\dfrac{11(6) - 6}{20}$

$\dfrac{66 - 6}{20}$

$\dfrac{60}{20}$

3

Since the value is 3 in each case, we have verified that $\dfrac{3x + 2}{4} - \dfrac{x + 4}{5} = \dfrac{11x - 6}{20}$.

3 Factorising

Factorising and simplifying expressions

There are four types of factorising that we will meet on this course:

Take out the common terms	Factorising by grouping
$ab + ad = a(b + d)$	$ab + ad + cb + cd = (a + c)(b + d)$
Factorise a trinomial (three terms)	**Difference of two squares**
$a^2 - 2ab + b^2 = (a - b)(a - b)$	$a^2 - b^2 = (a + b)(a - b)$

exam focus

Factorising is a basic and vital skill for you to have throughout your maths course. You must be able to factorise expressions quickly and easily. This will take practice, but it is worthwhile spending time on.

Factorising is the reverse process of expanding brackets. You could use the box method to verify your factors.

	a	b
a	a^2	ab
$-b$	$-ab$	$-b^2$

$= a^2 - ab + ab - b^2$

$= a^2 - b^2$

1. Take out common terms

1. Find the highest common factor (HCF) of all the terms making up the expression. This is the biggest value (constants of variables) which divides into all terms evenly.
2. Put the HCF outside the brackets.
3. Divide each term by the HCF to find the factor inside the brackets.

Example

Factorise the following:

(i) $4x + 8$

(ii) $12ab + 9a$

Solution

(i) $4x + 8$ (HCF is 4)

    $4(? + ?)$ (take out the 4)

    $4(x + 2)$

(ii) $12ab + 9a$ (HCF is $3a$)

    $3a(? + ?)$ (take out the $3a$)

    $3a(4b + 3)$

Example

Factorise the following:

(i) $3p^2 + 6pq + 9p$

(ii) $2a^2b + 3ab^2$

Solution

(i) $3p^2 + 6pq + 9p$

    $3pp + 6pq + 9p$ (HCF is $3p$)

    $3p(p + 2q + 3)$ (factorise out $3p$)

(ii) $2a^2b + 3ab^2$

    $2aab + 3abb$ (HCF is ab)

    $ab(2a + 3b)$ (factorise out ab)

Factorise the following:

(i) $20xy - 4x^2$

(ii) $18a^3 + 24ab$

Solution

(i) $20xy - 4x^2$

    $20xy - 4xx$ (HCF is $4x$)

    $4x(5y - x)$ (factorise out $4x$)

(ii) $18a^3 + 24ab$

    $18aaa + 24ab$ (HCF is $6a$)

    $6a(3a^2 + 4b)$ (factorise out $6a$)

2. Factorising by grouping

Use this method when you have four terms with no common factor.

1. Group into pairs with a common factor.
2. Take out the HCF in each pair separately.
3. Take out the new common factor.

Example

Factorise the following:

(i) $3a - 3b + ac - bc$

(ii) $3pr - 3ps + qr - qs$

Solution

(i) $3a - 3b + ac - bc$ (already in pairs with a common factor)

  $3(a - b) + c(a - b)$ (take out the common factor, in each pair)

  $(a - b)(3 + c)$ (take out the common factor $(a - b)$)

(ii) $3pr - 3ps + qr - qs$ (already in pairs with a common factor)

  $3p(r - s) + q(r - s)$ (take out the common factor, in each pair)

  $(r - s)(3p + q)$ (take out the common factor $(r - s)$)

Example

Factorise the following:

(i) $7b - cb + 7c - c^2$

(ii) $6p - 2c + 3pc - c^2$

Solution

(i) $7b - cb + 7c - c^2$ (already in pairs with a common factor)

  $b(7 - c) + c(7 - c)$ (take out the common factor in each pair)

  $(7 - c)(b + c)$ (take out the common factor $(7 - c)$)

(ii) $6p - 2c + 3pc - c^2$ (already in pairs with a common factor)

  $2(3p - c) + c(3p - c)$ (take out the common factor in each pair)

  $(3p - c)(2 + c)$ (take out the common factor $(3p - c)$)

Factorise the following:

(i) $3xy - 10x - 10b + 3by$

(ii) $4c^2 - 3d - 2cd + 6c$

Solution

(i) $3xy - 10x - 10b + 3by$ (already in pairs with a common factor)

    $x(3y - 10) + b(-10 + 3y)$ (take out the common factor in each pair)

    $x(3y - 10) + b(3y - 10)$ (reorder the second bracket)

    $(3y - 10)(x + b)$ (take out the common factor $(3y - 10)$)

(ii) $4c^2 - 3d - 2cd + 6c$ (no common factors in the first pair. Need to rearrange.)

    $4c^2 - 2cd + 6c - 3d$ (rearrange order of the terms so that they are grouped into pairs with a common factor)

    $2c(2c - d) + 3(2c - d)$ (take out the common factor in each pair)

    $(2c - d)(2c + 3)$ (take out the common factor $(2c - d)$)

The sign is part of the term directly after it. Take care when rearranging the terms. Keep the sign with each term.

3. Quadratic trinomials

An expression in the form $x^2 + bx + c$, where b and c are numbers, is called a quadratic trinomial. This is because in the expression, the highest power of x is 2 (quadratic) and it contains three terms (trinomial).

For factorising, quadratic trinomials can be broken into two types:

1. **Final term is positive**

   When the final term is positive, the signs inside the middle of the brackets will be the **same**, either two pluses or two minuses. Keep the sign of the middle term given in the question.

2. **Final term is negative**

   When the final term is negative, the signs inside the middle of the brackets will be **different**. (i.e. one positive and one negative).

Some quadratic trinomials can be very challenging to factorise. Do not be discouraged! If you cannot find the correct factors straight away, keep going until you have tried all options.

Example

Factorise $x^2 + 8x + 15$.

Solution

$x^2 + 8x + 15$ (final term, $+15$, is positive, so the signs in the brackets are the same)

$(x + 3)(x + 5)$

Check: outside terms $= (x)(5) = 5x$

inside terms $= (3)(x) = \underline{3x}$

sum $= \qquad 8x =$ middle term of original quadratic trinomial

Therefore, factors $(x + 3)(x + 5)$ are correct.

Use trial and improvement to find the factors. Multiply the inside terms, multiply the outside terms and add the results to see if you get the middle term of the original quadratic trinomial.

Check your answers:

	x	3
x	x^2	$3x$
5	$5x$	15

$= x^2 + 5x + 3x + 15$

$= x^2 + 8x + 15$

Alternative method:

$1x^2 + 8x + 15 \qquad 1 \times 15 = 15$ (15 is the guide number: it tells you that

M　　A　　M　　　　　　　　　both signs are the same)

We need factors of 15 which add to give 8.

M = 15	A = 8
$1 \times 15 = 15$	$1 + 15 = 16$
$3 \times 5 = 15$	$3 + 5 = 8$

Check these values on a calculator if you are not confident with integers.

The factors which fit this criteria are 3 and 5.

Rewrite the trinomial, replacing $8x$ with $3x$ and $5x$.

$1x^2 + 3x + 5x + 15$

$x(x + 3) + 5(x + 3)$ (factorise by grouping)

$(x + 3)(x + 5)$

Example

Factorise $x^2 - 7x + 10$.

Solution

$x^2 - 7x + 10$ (final term, $+10$, is positive, so the signs in the brackets are the same)

$(x - 2)(x - 5)$

Check: outside terms $= (x)(-5) = -5x$

inside terms $= (-2)(x) = \underline{-2x}$

sum $= \qquad\qquad -7x =$ middle term of original quadratic trinomial

Therefore, factors $(x - 2)(x - 5)$ are correct.

Check your answers:

	x	-2
x	x^2	$-2x$
-5	$-5x$	10

$= x^2 - 2x - 5x + 10$

$= x^2 - 7x + 10$

Alternative method:

$1x^2 - 7x + 10 \qquad 1 \times 10 = 10$ (10 is the guide number: it tells you that
M   A   M   both signs are the same)

We need factors of 10 which add to give -7.

M = 10	A = -7
$1 \times 10 = 10$	$1 + 10 = 11$
$2 \times 5 = 10$	$2 + 5 = 7$
$-2 \times -5 = 10$	$-2 - 5 = -7$

The factors which fit this criteria are -2 and -5.

Rewrite the trinomial, replacing $-7x$ with $-2x$ and $-5x$.

$1x^2 - 2x - 5x + 10$

$x(x - 2) - 5(x - 2)$ (factorise by grouping)

$(x - 2)(x - 5)$

Example

Factorise $x^2 + 2x - 8$.

Solution

$x^2 + 2x - 8$ (final term, -8, is negative, so the signs in the brackets are different)

$(x + 4)(x - 2)$

Check: outside terms $= (x)(-2) = -2x$

inside terms $= (4)(x) = \underline{4x}$

sum $= 2x =$ middle term of original quadratic trinomial

Therefore, factors $(x + 4)(x - 2)$ are correct.

Check your answers:

	x	4
x	x^2	$4x$
-2	$-2x$	-8

$= x^2 + 4x - 2x - 8$

$= x^2 + 2x - 8$

Alternative method:

$1x^2 + 2x - 8$ $\qquad$ $1 \times -8 = -8$ $\qquad$ (-8 is the guide number: it tells you that

M $\quad$ A $\quad$ M $\qquad\qquad\qquad\qquad\qquad$ the signs are different)

We need factors of -8 which add to give $+2$.

M = -8	A = 2
$1 \times -8 = -8$	$1 - 8 = -7$
$-1 \times 8 = -8$	$-1 + 8 = 7$
$-2 \times 4 = -8$	$-2 + 4 = 2$
$2 \times -4 = -8$	$2 - 4 = -2$

The factors which fit this criteria are 4 and -2.

Rewrite the trinomial, replacing $2x$ with $4x$ and $-2x$.

$1x^2 + 4x - 2x - 8$

$x(x + 4) - 2(x + 4)$ (factorise by grouping)

$(x + 4)(x - 2)$

Example

Factorise $x^2 - x - 12$.

Solution

$x^2 - x - 12$ (final term, -12, is negative, so the signs in the brackets are different)

$(x - 4)(x + 3)$

Check: outside terms $= (x)(3)$ $=$ $3x$

inside terms $= (-4)(x) = \underline{-4x}$

sum $=$ $-x =$ middle term of original quadratic trinomial

Therefore, factors $(x - 4)(x + 3)$ are correct.

Check your answers:

	x	-4
x	x^2	$-4x$
3	$3x$	-12

$= x^2 - 4x + 3x - 12$

$= x^2 - x - 12$

Alternative method:

$1x^2 - x - 12$ $1 \times -12 = -12$ (-12 is the guide number: it tells you that
M   A   M   the signs are different)

We need factors of -12 which add to give -1.

M = -12	A = -1
$1 \times -12 = -12$	$1 - 12 = -11$
$-1 \times 12 = -12$	$-1 + 12 = 11$
$2 \times -6 = -12$	$2 - 6 = -4$
$-2 \times 6 = -12$	$-2 + 6 = 4$
$3 \times -4 = -12$	$3 - 4 = -1$
$-3 \times 4 = -12$	$-3 + 4 = 1$

The factors which fit this criteria are -4 and 3.

Rewrite the trinomial, replacing $-x$ with $-4x$ and $3x$.

$1x^2 - 4x + 3x - 12$

$x(x - 4) + 3(x - 4)$ (factorise by grouping)

$(x - 4)(x + 3)$

4. Difference of two squares

An expression such as $a^2 - b^2$ is called the difference of two squares.

1. Write each term as a perfect square with brackets.
2. Use the rule $a^2 - b^2 = (a - b)(a + b)$

key point

The difference of two squares is a special case of a trinomial. $x^2 - 25$ can be written as $x^2 + 0x - 25$ and factorised as $(x + 5)(x - 5)$.

Example

Factorise the following:

  (i) $x^2 - 16$ (ii) $y^2 - 49$

Solution

(i) $x^2 - 16$

   $x^2 - (4)^2$

   $(x + 4)(x - 4)$

(ii) $y^2 - 49$

   $(y)^2 - (7)^2$

   $(y + 7)(y - 7)$

key point

Notice that the brackets are the same except for having opposite signs.

Example

Factorise the following:

(i) $p^2 - 64$

(ii) $3x^2 - 12$

Solution

(i) $p^2 - 64$

    $(p)^2 - (8)^2$

    $(p + 8)(p - 8)$

(ii) $3x^2 - 12$

    $3(x^2 - 4)$ (take out the common factor)

    $3(x^2 - (2)^2)$

    $3(x + 2)(x - 2)$

Preparing for the exam

You must practise the previous four different types of factorising and be able to recognise when to use each type. In the exam you may be given a number of expressions to factorise. It is up to you to know which method of factorising to use.

The following steps should help you to determine which type of factorising to use:

1. Check for common factors — if there are any, factorise these out.
2. Are there four terms for factorising by grouping?
3. Is it a quadratic trinomial, in the form $x^2 + bx + c$?
4. Are there only two terms? Are they squares? If so, use the difference of two squares.

Example

Factorise fully each of the following:

(i) $20xy - 4x^2$

(ii) $ax + 2ay + 3x + 6y$

Solution

(i) Take out common factors:

    $20xy - 4x^2$

    $20xy - 4xx$ (HCF is $4x$)

    $4x(5y - x)$

(ii) Factorise by grouping:

    $ax + 2ay + 3x + 6y$

    $a(x + 2y) + 3(x + 2y)$

    $(x + 2y)(a + 3)$

Factorise fully each of the following expressions:

  (i) $5x^3 - 10x^2$

  (ii) $x^2 - 81$

(iii) $a^2 - ab + 3a - 3b$

Solution

  (i) To factorise $5x^3 - 10x^2$, you must take out common factors.

     $5x^3 - 10x^2$

     $5xxx - 10xx$ (HCF is $5xx$)

     $5xx(x - 2)$ (factorise out $5xx$)

     $5x^2(x - 2)$ ($5xx = 5x^2$)

  (ii) To factorise $x^2 - 81$, you must find the difference of two squares.

     $x^2 - 81$

     $(x)^2 - (9)^2$

     $(x + 9)(x - 9)$

(iii) To factorise $a^2 - ab + 3a - 3b$,
you must factorise by grouping.

     $a^2 - ab + 3a - 3b$

     $aa - ab + 3a - 3b$

     $a(a - b) + 3(a - b)$

     $(a - b)(a + 3)$

As shown here, you may be asked to use different types of factorising in the one exam question. You must be able to recognise which type of factorising is needed in each case.

Factorise fully each of the following expressions:

  (i) $4xy - 6x^2y^2$

  (ii) $2ax - ay + 2bx - by$

Solution

(i) To factorise $4xy - 6x^2y^2$ you must take out common factors.

$4xy - 6x^2y^2$

$4xy - 6xxyy$ (HCF is $2xy$)

$2xy(2 - 3xy)$

(ii) To factorise $2ax - ay + 2bx - by$, you must factorise by grouping.

This question was worth 10 marks, with 8 marks awarded for correctly factorising either part **(i) or (ii)**.

$2ax - ay + 2bx - by$

$a(2x - y) + b(2x - y)$ (take the common factors out of each pair)

$(2x - y)(a + b)$ (take out the common factor $(2x - y)$)

(i) There are four terms given below. Three of them have a common factor other than 1.

    $3xy$ $6ay$ $11ax$ $9y$

Underline these three terms and write down the highest common factor of the three terms.

(ii) Factorise fully each of the following expressions:

    (a) $4x + 8y - 12z$ **(b)** $ab - 2a + 3b - 6$

    (c) $x^2 + 5x + 6$ **(d)** $b^2 - 16$

Solution

(i) The three terms which have a common factor other than 1 are underlined.

    <u>$3xy$</u>   <u>$6ay$</u> $11ax$ <u>$9y$</u>

The highest common factor of these three terms is $3y$.

(ii) Factorise each of the following.

    (a) To factorise $4x + 8y - 12z$, you must take out any common factors.

        $4x + 8y - 12z$ (HCF is 4)

        $4(x + 2y - 3z)$

(b) To factorise $ab - 2a + 3b - 6$, you must factorise by grouping.

$ab - 2a + 3b - 6$

$a(b - 2) + 3(b - 2)$ (take the common factors out of each pair)

$(b - 2)(a + 3)$ (take out the common factors $(b - 2)$)

(c) To factorise $x^2 + 5x + 6$, you must factorise a quadratic trinomial.

We need factors of 6 which add up to 5. These factors are 2 and 3.

$(x + 2)(x + 3)$

(d) To factorise $b^2 - 16$, you must factorise the difference of two squares.

$b^2 - (4)^2$

$(b + 4)(b - 4)$

exam focus

This question had five parts to answer. (Part **(i)** was taken as one part.)
The entire question was worth 10 marks.
8 marks were awarded for getting any three of the five parts correct.
7 marks were awarded for getting any one of the five parts correct.
5 marks were awarded for any correct attempt shown.
Make sure you attempt all questions. There are no marks for blanks!

exam Q

(i) Factorise $4x^2 - 12x$.

(ii) Factorise $x^2 - 6x + 9$.

(iii) Simplify $\dfrac{4x^2 - 12x}{x^2 - 6x + 9}$.

Solution

(i) $4x^2 - 12x$ (HCF is $4x$)

$4x(x - 3)$ (factorise out $4x$)

(ii) $x^2 - 6x + 9$

$(x - 3)(x - 3)$

(iii) $\dfrac{4x^2 - 12x}{x^2 - 6x + 9}$

$\dfrac{4x(x - 3)}{(x - 3)(x - 3)}$

$\dfrac{4x}{x - 3}$

Simplify $\dfrac{x^2 + x - 20}{3x - 12}$.

Solution

$\dfrac{(x + 5)(x - 4)}{3(x - 4)}$ (factorise the top and bottom)

$\dfrac{x + 5}{3}$ (divide the top and bottom by $(x - 4)$)

Simplify $\dfrac{x^2 + 7x + 12}{x^2 + 2x - 3}$.

Solution

$\dfrac{(x + 3)(x + 4)}{(x + 3)(x - 1)}$ (factorise the top and bottom)

$\dfrac{x + 4}{x - 1}$ (divide the top and bottom by $(x + 3)$)

4) Solving Linear Equations

☐ To learn how to solve linear equations.
☐ To learn how to form and solve linear equations in in-context questions.

An equation is solved with the following method:

> Whatever you do to one side, you must do exactly the same to the other side.

Note: Keep balance in mind.
The solution of an equation is the number that makes both sides balance.

Example

Find the value of x given that $2x - 7 = 23$.

Solution

$$2x - 7 = 23$$
$$2x - 7 + 7 = 23 + 7 \quad \text{(add 7 to both sides)}$$
$$2x = 30 \quad \text{(simplify)}$$
$$x = 15 \quad \text{(divide both sides by 2)}$$

Solve $3(x - 2) + 1 = 19$.

Solution

$$3(x - 2) + 1 = 19$$
$$3x - 6 + 1 = 19 \quad \text{(multiply out the brackets)}$$
$$3x - 5 = 19 \quad \text{(simplify)}$$
$$3x - 5 + 5 = 19 + 5 \quad \text{(add 5 to both sides)}$$
$$3x = 24 \quad \text{(simplify)}$$
$$x = 8 \quad \text{(divide both sides by 3)}$$

Example

Solve the equation: $-2(x - 3) = 10$.

Take care when multiplying negative terms: $(-2)(-3) = +6$.

Solution

$$-2(x - 3) = 10$$
$$-2x + 6 = 10 \qquad \text{(multiply out)}$$
$$-2x + 6 - 6 = 10 - 6 \qquad \text{(subtract 6 from both sides)}$$
$$-2x = 4 \qquad \text{(simplify)}$$
$$x = -2 \qquad \text{(divide both sides by } -2)$$

Example

Solve the equation $3(x - 2) = 2x + 5$.

Solution

$$3(x - 2) = 2x + 5$$
$$3x - 6 = 2x + 5 \qquad \text{(remove brackets)}$$
$$3x - 6 + 6 = 2x + 5 + 6 \qquad \text{(add 6 to both sides)}$$
$$3x = 2x + 11 \qquad \text{(simplify)}$$
$$3x - 2x = 2x + 11 - 2x \qquad \text{(subtract } 2x \text{ from both sides)}$$
$$x = 11 \qquad \text{(simplify)}$$

Solve the equation $3(2x - 7) = 5(x - 1)$.

Solution

$$3(2x - 7) = 5(x - 1)$$
$$6x - 21 = 5x - 5 \qquad \text{(remove brackets)}$$
$$6x - 21 - 5x = 5x - 5 - 5x \qquad \text{(subtract } 5x \text{ from both sides)}$$
$$x - 21 = -5 \qquad \text{(simplify)}$$
$$x - 21 + 21 = -5 + 21 \qquad \text{(add 21 to both sides)}$$
$$x = 16 \qquad \text{(add 21 to both sides)}$$

Solve the equation $5(3x + 1) - 2(5x + 35) = 0$.

Verify your answer.

Solution

$5(3x + 1) - 2(5x + 35) = 0$

$15x + 5 - 10x - 70 = 0$	(remove brackets)
$5x - 65 = 0$	(simplify)
$5x - 65 + 65 = 65$	(add 65 to both sides)
$5x = 65$	(simplify)
$x = \dfrac{65}{5}$	(divide both sides by 5)
$x = 13$	

To verify your answer, let $x = 13$ in the original equation:

$$5(3x + 1) - 2(5x + 35) = 0$$
$$5(3(13) + 1) - 2(5(13) + 35) = 0$$
$$5(39 + 1) - 2(65 + 35) = 0$$
$$5(40) - 2(100) = 0$$
$$200 - 200 = 0$$
$$0 = 0$$

The equation is balanced, therefore we have verified our answer.

Real-life applications to solving equations

You will often be required to solve an equation which has been given in a real-world situation. These are also called in-context problems.

These real-life applications can appear in various topics throughout your course. Be aware that these questions may not always look like algebra.

Example

Zach drove from Town A to Town B, a distance of x km.

He then drove from Town B to Town C, a distance of $(2x + 1)$ km.

The total distance that he drove was 55km. Find the value of x.

Hence, find the distance between Town A and Town B and also Town B and Town C.

Solution

Total distance = (Town A to Town B) + (Town B to Town C)

$$55 = (x) + (2x + 1)$$
$$55 = x + 2x + 1 \quad \text{(remove brackets)}$$
$$55 = 3x + 1 \quad \text{(simplify)}$$
$$55 - 1 = 3x + 1 - 1 \quad \text{(subtract 1 from both sides)}$$
$$54 = 3x \quad \text{(simplify)}$$
$$18 = x \quad \text{(divide both sides by 3)}$$

Writing the equation in words first can be helpful.

Town A to Town B = xm = 18km

Town B to Town C = $2x + 1 = 2(18) + 1 = 36 + 1 = 37$km

Example

Amy has €x. James has €6 more than Amy.

(i) How much money does James have, in terms of x?

(ii) If Amy and James have €16 in total, write an equation in x to show this information.

(iii) Solve the equation to find how much money Amy has.

Solution

(i) James has €6 more than Amy.

James has €$(6 + x)$.

(ii) Amy + James = 16

$$x + (6 + x) = 16$$

(iii) Solve:

'in terms of x' means that the variable x must be in your answer.

$$x + (6 + x) = 16$$
$$x + 6 + x = 16 \quad \text{(remove brackets)}$$
$$2x + 6 = 16 \quad \text{(simplify)}$$
$$2x + 6 - 6 = 16 - 6 \quad \text{(subtract 6 from both sides)}$$
$$2x = 10 \quad \text{(simplify)}$$
$$x = 5 \quad \text{(divide both sides by 2)}$$

Therefore, Amy has €5.

Example

(i) Eoin is t years of age.

Katie is 4 years older than Eoin.

Laura is twice as old as Eoin.

Write Katie's age and Laura's age in terms of t.

(ii) From part (i), the sum of Eoin's age, Katie's age and Laura's age is 52.

Write down an equation in t to represent this information.

(iii) Solve your equation to find Eoin's age in years.

Solution

(i) Eoin is t years of age.

Katie is 4 years older than Eoin. Therefore, Katie is $(t + 4)$ years old.

Laura is twice as old as Eoin. Therefore, Laura is $(2t)$ years old.

(ii) (Eoin's age) + (Katie's age) + (Laura's age) = 52

$$(t) + (t + 4) + (2t) = 52$$

(iii) Solve $(t) + (t + 4) + (2t) = 52$

$t + t + 4 + 2t = 52$	(remove brackets)
$4t + 4 = 52$	(simplify)
$4t + 4 - 4 = 52 - 4$	(subtract 4 from both sides)
$4t = 48$	(simplify)
$t = 12$	(divide both sides by 4)

Therefore, Eoin is 12 years old.

(i) The cost of a DVD is €x. The cost of a CD is €3 less.

What is the cost of a CD in terms of x?

(ii) The total cost of three DVDs and two CDs is €54.

Write an equation in x to represent this information.

(iii) Solve your equation to find the cost of a DVD.

Solution

(i) DVD = €x

CD = cost of DVD − 3

CD = €$(x − 3)$

(ii) The total cost of three DVDs and two CDs is €54.

$3(x) + 2(x - 3) = 54$

(iii) Solve: $3(x) + 2(x - 3) = 54$

$$3x + 2x - 6 = 54 \quad \text{(remove brackets)}$$
$$5x - 6 = 54 \quad \text{(simplify)}$$
$$5x - 6 + 6 = 54 + 6 \quad \text{(add 6 to both sides)}$$
$$5x = 60 \quad \text{(simplify)}$$
$$x = 12 \quad \text{(divide both sides by 5)}$$

Hence a DVD costs €12

(i) Conor spent €y on a book. He then spent €$(4y + 6)$ on a football jersey. In total, he spent €61.

Write an equation in y to represent this information.

(ii) Solve your equation from **(i)** to find the value of y.

(iii) Hence, find the cost of the book and the cost of the football jersey that Conor bought.

Solution

(i) Book + Football jersey = €61

$$(y) + (4y + 6) = 61$$

(ii) Solve: $(y) + (4y + 6) = 61$

$$y + 4y + 6 = 61 \quad \text{(remove brackets)}$$
$$5y + 6 = 61$$
$$5y = 61 - 6 \quad \text{(subtract 6 from both sides)}$$
$$5y = 55$$
$$y = \frac{55}{5} \quad \text{(divide both sides by 5)}$$
$$y = 11$$

(iii) Book: €y = €11

Jersey: €$4y + 6$ = €$4(11) + 6$ = €$44 + 6$ = €50

Clodagh tests the knowledge of her two younger sisters, Anna and Lauren.

(i) Clodagh says that the sum of two consecutive numbers is 35. Anna answers that the numbers are 20 and 15. Lauren says that the numbers are 17 and 18.

Which sister is right? Give a reason for your answer.

(ii) Clodagh then says, 'When 8 is added to three times a number, the result is 47'.

Anna works out the correct answer, which is 13.

Show one method Anna could have used to get the correct answer.

key point

Consecutive means one after another

Solution

(i) Anna is incorrect, as although the sum of the numbers 20 and 15 is 35, the numbers are not consecutive numbers.

Lauren is correct, as the sum of the numbers 17 and 18 is 35, and the numbers are consecutive numbers.

(ii) Let the number be x:

When 8 is added to three times a number, the result is 47.

$$8 + 3x = 47$$
$$8 + 3x - 8 = 47 - 8 \qquad \text{(subtract 8 from both sides)}$$
$$3x = 39 \qquad \text{(simplify)}$$
$$x = 13 \qquad \text{(divide both sides by 3)}$$

exam focus

Part **(i)** was worth 5 marks, with 3 marks awarded for partial credit, for example giving the correct answer with an incorrect reason, or an incorrect answer but the correct reason.

Part **(ii)** was worth 5 marks, with 3 marks awarded for partial credit.

Jane sets Molly a word problem. 'If I multiply a number by 7 and add 4, the result is the same as multiplying the number by 3 and taking away 8.' Molly starts by writing $7x + 4 =$.

Finish Molly's equation and solve it to find the number.

Solution

Letting the number be x:

Multiply a number by 7 and add 4. The result is the same as multiplying the number by 3 and taking away 8.

$$7x + 4 = 3x - 8$$

$7x + 4 - 3x = 3x - 8 - 3x$	(subtract $3x$ from both sides)
$4x + 4 = -8$	(simplify)
$4x + 4 - 4 = -8 - 4$	(subtract 4 from both sides)
$4x = -12$	(simplify)
$\dfrac{4x}{4} = \dfrac{-12}{4}$	(divide both sides by 4)
$x = -3$	

This exam question was not well answered by candidates. Consequently, the entire question was worth 2 marks. One mark was awarded for correctly completing the equation and the second mark was awarded for solving the equation.

x is a number. A second number is 5 greater than x.

(i) Write down the second number in terms of x.

(ii) Twice the first number added to three times the second number is equal to 35. Write down an equation in x to represent this information.

(iii) Solve your equation for x and state what the two numbers are.

(iv) Verify your result.

Solution

(i) A second number is 5 greater than x, therefore the second number is $x + 5$.

(ii) Twice the first number added to three times the second number is equal to 35.

$$2(\text{first number}) + 3(\text{second number}) = 35$$
$$2(x) + 3(x + 5) = 35$$

(iii) Solve: $2(x) + 3(x + 5) = 35$

$$2x + 3x + 15 = 35 \qquad \text{(remove brackets)}$$
$$5x + 15 = 35 \qquad \text{(simplify)}$$
$$5x + 15 - 15 = 35 - 15 \qquad \text{(subtract 15 from both sides)}$$
$$5x = 20 \qquad \text{(simplify)}$$
$$x = 4 \qquad \text{(divide both sides by 5)}$$

First number $= x = 4$

Second number $= x + 5 = 4 + 5 = 9$

(iv) To verify the results, see if 2(first number) + 3(second number) = 35

$$2(\text{first number}) + 3(\text{second number})$$
$$2(4) + 3(9)$$
$$8 + 27$$
$$35$$

Therefore, we have verified our results.

The length of a rectangle is $(3x + 11)$ units and the width is $(5x - 23)$ units, as shown in the diagram.

(i) Find, in terms of x, the perimeter of the rectangle.

(ii) If the perimeter is 88 units, find x.

Solution

(i) Perimeter $= 2(\text{Length}) + 2(\text{Width})$
$$= 2(3x + 11) + 2(5x - 23)$$
$$= 6x + 22 + 10x - 46$$
$$= 16x - 24$$

(ii) Perimeter $= 88$

Perimeter $= 16x - 24$
$$88 = 16x - 24$$
$$88 + 24 = 16x \quad \text{(add 24 to both sides)}$$
$$112 = 16x$$
$$7 = x \quad \text{(divide both sides by 16)}$$

Equations with fractions

If there are fractions in an equation, multiply all parts by a number that all of the denominators divide evenly into. This number is known as the common denominator.

Example

Solve the equation $\frac{1}{2}(7x - 2) + 5 = 2x + 7$.

Solution

$$\frac{1}{2}(7x - 2) + 5 = 2x + 7$$

$2\left(\frac{1}{2}(7x - 2)\right) + 2(5) = 2(2x) + 2(7)$	(multiply each term by 2)
$1(7x - 2) + 2(5) = 2(2x) + 2(7)$	(since $2 \times \frac{1}{2} = 1$)
$7x - 2 + 10 = 4x + 14$	(multiply out the brackets)
$7x + 8 = 4x + 14$	(simplify)
$7x + 8 - 4x = 4x + 14 - 4x$	(subtract $4x$ from both sides)
$3x + 8 = 14$	(simplify)
$3x + 8 - 8 = 14 - 8$	(subtract 8 from both sides)
$3x = 6$	(simplify)
$x = 2$	(divide both sides by 3)

key point

You cannot apply the method of multiplying all parts by a number unless the expression is an equation. That is, it must have an equals (=) sign.

Example

Solve the equation $\dfrac{x - 7}{2} = \dfrac{x + 3}{6}$.

Solution

$$\frac{x - 7}{2} = \frac{x + 3}{6}$$

$$6\left(\frac{x - 7}{2}\right) = 6\left(\frac{x + 3}{6}\right) \quad \text{(multiply each term by 6)}$$

$$3(x - 7) = 1(x + 3) \qquad \text{(divide the denominators into the LCM)}$$
$$3x - 21 = x + 3 \qquad \text{(multiply out the brackets)}$$
$$3x - 21 - x = x + 3 - x \qquad \text{(subtract } x \text{ from both sides)}$$
$$2x - 21 = 3 \qquad \text{(simplify)}$$
$$2x - 21 + 21 = 3 + 21 \qquad \text{(add 21 to both sides)}$$
$$2x = 24 \qquad \text{(simplify)}$$
$$x = 12 \qquad \text{(divide both sides by 2)}$$

Solve the equation $\dfrac{3(x + 3)}{4} - \dfrac{2(x - 3)}{3} = \dfrac{x + 1}{2}$.

Solution

$$\frac{3(x + 3)}{4} - \frac{2(x - 3)}{3} = \frac{x + 1}{2} \qquad \text{(the LCM of 4, 3 and 2 is 12)}$$

$$12\left(\frac{3(x + 3)}{4}\right) - 12\left(\frac{2(x - 3)}{3}\right) = 12\left(\frac{x + 1}{2}\right) \qquad \text{(multiply each term by the LCM, 12)}$$

$$3(3(x + 3)) - 4(2(x - 3)) = 6(x + 1) \qquad \text{(divide the denominators into the LCM)}$$

$$9(x + 3) - 8(x - 3) = 6(x + 1)$$

$$9x + 27 - 8x + 24 = 6x + 6 \qquad \text{(multiply out the brackets)}$$

$$x + 51 = 6x + 6 \qquad \text{(simplify)}$$

$$x + 51 - x = 6x + 6 - x \qquad \text{(subtract x from both sides)}$$

$$51 = 5x + 6 \qquad \text{(simplify)}$$

$$51 - 6 = 5x + 6 - 6 \qquad \text{(subtract 6 from both sides)}$$

$$45 = 5x \qquad \text{(simplify)}$$

$$9 = x \qquad \text{(divide both sides by 5)}$$

(i) Express $\dfrac{2x - 1}{5} + \dfrac{x + 7}{2}$ as a single fraction.
Give your answer in its simplest form.

(ii) Hence or otherwise, solve the equation
$$\frac{2x - 1}{5} + \frac{x + 7}{2} = 6.$$

Solution

(i) $\dfrac{2x - 1}{5} + \dfrac{x + 7}{2}$ (common denominator is 10)

$\dfrac{2(2x - 1) + 5(x + 7)}{10}$

$\dfrac{4x - 2 + 5x + 35}{10}$

$\dfrac{9x + 33}{10}$

(ii) $\dfrac{2x - 1}{5} + \dfrac{x + 7}{2} = 6$

$\dfrac{9x + 33}{10} = 6$ (from **(i)**)

$10\left(\dfrac{9x + 33}{10}\right) = 10(6)$ (multiply both sides by the LCM, 10)

$9x + 33 = 60$

$9x + 33 - 33 = 60 - 33$ (subtract 33 from both sides)

$9x = 27$ (simplify)

$x = 3$ (divide both sides by 9)

key point

We cannot multiply across by a number in part (i) because this expression is not an equation. Adding algebraic fractions was covered in an earlier chapter.

exam Q

The three angles of a triangle are $\dfrac{8(x - 2)}{3}, \; 4x + 7, \; \dfrac{5x - 10}{2}$.

Find the value of x.

exam focus

Notice the link between Geometry and Algebra in this question.

Solution

The three angles of a triangle sum to 180°.

$$\left(\dfrac{8(x - 2)}{3}\right) + (4x + 7) + \left(\dfrac{5x - 10}{2}\right) = 180$$

$6\left(\dfrac{8(x - 2)}{3}\right) + 6(4x + 7) + 6\left(\dfrac{5x - 10}{2}\right) = 6(180)$ (multiply each term by the LCM, 6)

$2(8(x - 2)) + 6(4x + 7) + 3(5x - 10) = 6(180)$ (divide the denominators into LCM)

$16(x - 2) + 24x + 42 + 15x - 30 = 1{,}080$ (multiply out the brackets)

$16x - 32 + 39x + 12 = 1{,}080$ (simplify)

$55x - 20 = 1{,}080$

$55x = 1{,}100$ (add 20 to both sides)

$x = 20$ (divide both sides by 55)

5 Solving Quadratic Equations

aims
- ☐ To learn how to solve a quadratic equation when given in different forms.
- ☐ To be able to solve quadratic equations when they appear during in-context questions.

Any equation of the form $x^2 + bx + c = 0$ is called a quadratic equation. Solving a quadratic equation gives us the roots of the equation. These are the two values which satisfy the equation.

To solve a quadratic equation: factorise the expression then let each factor equal zero and solve.

key point

There are three different types of quadratic equation. It is vital for you to remember and be familiar with how to factorise each type. Methods of factorising were covered in an earlier chapter. It would be wise to revise these methods before continuing with this chapter.

Take out common terms	Difference of two squares	Factorise a trinomial
$x^2 + 2x = x(x + 2)$	$x^2 - 9 = (x + 3)(x - 3)$	$x^2 + 6x - 7 = (x - 1)(x + 7)$

Example

Solve the following quadratic equation: $2x^2 + 6x = 0$.

Solution

$$2x^2 + 6x = 0$$
$$2x(x + 3) = 0 \quad \text{(factorise: take out common factors)}$$
$$2x = 0 \quad \text{or} \quad x + 3 = 0 \quad \text{(let each factor equal zero)}$$
$$x = 0 \quad \text{or} \quad x = -3 \quad \text{(solve)}$$

key point

These values for x are called the roots of the quadratic equation. These values are the points where the graph of the quadratic function crosses the x-axis. This is covered in further detail in the chapter on graphing functions.

Example

Solve the following quadratic equation: $x^2 - 81 = 0$.

Solution

$$x^2 - 81 = 0$$
$$(x + 9)(x - 9) = 0 \quad \text{(factorise: difference of two squares)}$$
$$x + 9 = 0 \quad \text{or} \quad x - 9 = 0 \quad \text{(let each factor equal zero)}$$
$$x = -9 \text{ or} \quad x = 9 \quad \text{(solve)}$$

Example

Solve the following quadratic equation: $x^2 + 2x - 15 = 0$.

Solution

Factorise the quadratic trinomial on the left-hand side:

$x^2 + 2x - 15$ (final term, -15, is negative, so the signs in the brackets are different)

$(x + 5)(x - 3)$

Check: outside terms $= (x)(-3) = -3x$

       inside terms $= (5)(x) \quad = \quad \underline{5x}$

           sum $= \qquad\qquad 2x =$ middle term of original quadratic trinomial

Therefore, factors $(x + 5)(x - 3)$ are correct.

$$x^2 + 2x - 15 = 0$$
$$(x + 5)(x - 3) = 0 \quad \text{(factorise: quadratic trinomial)}$$
$$x + 5 = 0 \quad \text{or} \quad x - 3 = 0 \quad \text{(let each factor equal zero)}$$
$$x = -5 \text{ or} \qquad x = 3 \quad \text{(solve)}$$

It is a good idea to check your solutions in the original equation. In this example:

$x = -5$: $(-5)^2 + 2(-5) - 15$	$x = 3$: $(3)^2 + 2(3) - 15$
$= 25 - 10 - 15$	$= 9 + 6 - 15$
$= 0$	$= 0$
$\therefore x = -5$ is a solution	$\therefore x = 3$ is a solution

Solve the following quadratic equations:

(i) $x^2 - 5x - 6 = 0$ **(ii)** $x^2 + 7x - 18 = 0$

Solution

(i) $\qquad\qquad x^2 - 5x - 6 = 0$

$\qquad\qquad\quad (x - 6)(x + 1) = 0$ (factorise: quadratic trinomial)

$\qquad x - 6 = 0 \quad \text{or} \quad x + 1 = 0$

$\qquad\quad x = 6 \quad \text{or} \qquad x = -1$

(ii) $\qquad\qquad x^2 + 7x - 18 = 0$

$\qquad\qquad\quad (x + 9)(x - 2) = 0$ (factorise)

$\qquad x + 9 = 0 \quad \text{or} \quad x - 2 = 0$

$\qquad\quad x = -9 \quad \text{or} \qquad x = 2$

(i) Factorise $x^2 - 13x + 36$.

(ii) Hence, solve $x^2 - 13x + 36 = 0$.

Solution

(i) $x^2 - 13x + 36$

$\quad (x - 4)(x - 9)$ (factorise: quadratic trinomial)

(ii) $\qquad\qquad x^2 - 13x + 36 = 0$

$\qquad\qquad\quad (x - 4)(x - 9) = 0$

$\qquad x - 4 = 0 \quad \text{or} \quad x - 9 = 0$

$\qquad\quad x = 4 \quad \text{or} \qquad x = 9$

Remember, 'Hence' in part **(ii)** means that you **must** use your solution from **(i)**.

Example

The sides of a right-angled triangle are $3x$, $4x$ and $5x$ in length. The area of the triangle is 216 square units. Use this information to write an equation in x.

Solve the equation and hence find the lengths of the sides of the triangle.

Solution

Area of a triangle $= \dfrac{1}{2}(\text{Base})(\perp \text{Height})$

$$216 = \dfrac{1}{2}(4x)(3x)$$

Write the formula and fill in the information from the question. Then solve the equation to find the remaining variable.

$$2(216) = 2\left[\dfrac{1}{2}(4x)(3x)\right] \qquad \text{(multiply both sides by 2)}$$

$$432 = 12x^2$$

$$\dfrac{432}{12} = x^2 \qquad \text{(divide both sides by 12)}$$

$$36 = x^2$$

$$0 = x^2 - 36 \qquad \text{(subtract 36 from both sides)}$$

$$0 = (x + 6)(x - 6) \qquad \text{(factorise: difference of two squares)}$$

$$x + 6 = 0 \quad \text{or} \quad x - 6 = 0 \qquad \text{(let each factor equal zero)}$$

$x = -6$ | $x = 6$

Reject, as length can't be negative | Accept

If you get more than one answer it is important to look at which solutions make sense. Apply logic to determine which answers, if any, to reject.

Sides are: $3x = 3(6) = 18$ units

$4x = 4(6) = 24$ units

$5x = 5(6) = 30$ units

A car is moving away from a wall. The distance, S, in metres between the car and the wall, after t seconds, is given by:

$$S = t^2 + 5t + 12.$$

(i) How far is the car from the wall after 3 seconds?

|←——— Distance, S ———→|

(ii) How far is the car from the wall after 8 seconds?

(iii) After how many seconds is the car a distance of 48m from the wall?

Solution

(i) Find S when $t = 3$: $S = t^2 + 5t + 12$

$$S = (3)^2 + 5(3) + 12$$
$$S = 9 + 15 + 12 = 36$$

Therefore, the car has travelled 36m after 3 seconds.

This is also a functions question. These are covered in detail in the chapter on functions.

(ii) Find S when $t = 8$: $S = t^2 + 5t + 12$

$$S = (8)^2 + 5(8) + 12$$
$$S = 64 + 40 + 12 = 116$$

Therefore, the car has travelled 116m after 8 seconds.

(iii) Find t when $S = 48$: $S = t^2 + 5t + 12$

$$48 = t^2 + 5t + 12$$
$$48 - 48 = t^2 + 5t + 12 - 48$$
$$0 = t^2 + 5t - 36$$
$$0 = (t - 4)(t + 9) \qquad \text{(factorise: quadratic trinomial)}$$

$$t - 4 = 0 \quad \text{or} \quad t + 9 = 0$$
$$t = 4 \quad \text{or} \quad t = -9$$

Accept   Reject, as you can't have a negative time

Therefore, after 4 seconds the car is 48m from the wall.

6 Simultaneous Equations

☐ To learn how to use suitable strategies for finding solutions to simultaneous linear equations with two unknowns.

☐ To learn how to interpret the results from solving two equations simultaneously.

Simultaneous linear equations with two unknowns

Simultaneous linear equations in two variables are solved with the following steps:

1. Write both equations in the form $ax + by = k$ and label the equations ① and ②.
2. Multiply one or both of the equations by a number in order to make the coefficients of x or y the same, but of opposite sign.
3. Add to remove the variable with equal coefficients but of opposite sign.
4. Solve the resultant equation to find the value of the remaining unknown (x or y).
5. Substitute this value in equation ① or ② to find the value of the other unknown.

Note: When there are two unknown variables we must have two equations.

Example

Solve the following pair of simultaneous equations:

$$2x + y = 72 \quad \text{and} \quad x - y = -27.$$

Solution

To eliminate the y's:

Step 1: ① $2x + y = 72$

    ② $\underline{x - y = -27}$ (add the rows)

Step 3: $3x = 45$ ($\div 3$)

Step 4: $x = 15$

To find the value for y, let $x = 15$ in either of the equations:

Step 5: ① $2x + y = 72$

     $2(15) + y = 72$

     $30 + y = 72$

      $y = 42$

Therefore, the solution is $x = 15, y = 42$.

Note: Step 2 wasn't needed in this example.

Example

Solve the following pair of simultaneous equations:

$2p + 3q = 5$ and $p - 4q = -14$.

Equations do not always have to be in terms of x and y.

Solution

To eliminate the p's:

Step 1: ① $\quad 2p + 3q = 5$

② $\quad\quad p - 4q = -14 \quad (\times -2)$

Step 2: ① $\quad 2p + 3q = 5$

② $\quad -2p + 8q = 28 \quad$ (add the rows)

Step 3: $\quad\quad\quad 11q = 33 \quad (\div 11)$

Step 4: $\quad\quad\quad\quad q = 3$

To find the value for p, let $q = 3$ in either of the equations:

Step 5: ① $\quad 2p + 3q = 5$

$2p + 3(3) = 5$

$2p + 9 = 5$

$2p = -4$

$p = -2$

Therefore, the solution is $p = -2, q = 3$.

Solve the following pair of simultaneous equations:

$5a + b = 1$ and $2a + 3b = -10$.

Solution

To eliminate the b's:

Step 1: ① $\quad\quad 5a + b = 1 \quad\quad (\times -3)$

② $\quad\quad 2a + 3b = -10$

Step 2: ① $-15a - 3b = -3$

② $\quad\quad 2a + 3b = -10 \quad$ (add the rows)

Step 3: $-13a \quad\quad\quad = -13 \quad (\div -13)$

Step 4: $\quad\quad\quad\quad a = 1$

Therefore, solution is $a = 1, b = -4$.

To find the value for b, let $a = 1$ in either of the equations:

Step 5: ① $\quad 5a + b = 1$

$5(1) + b = 1$

$5 + b = 1$

$b = -4$

Solve the following pair of simultaneous equations:

$$3x + 5y = 13 \quad \text{and} \quad x + 2y = 5.$$

Solution

To eliminate the x's:

Step 1: ① $3x + 5y = 13$

 ② $\underline{x + 2y = 5}$ $\quad (\times -3)$

Step 2: ① $3x + 5y = 13$

 ② $\underline{-3x - 6y = -15}$ (add the rows)

Step 3: $\qquad -y = -2$ $\quad (\div -1)$

Step 4: $\qquad y = 2$

Therefore, the solution is $x = 1$, $y = 2$.

To find the value for x, let $y = 2$ in either of the equations:

Step 5: ② $x + 2y = 5$

$x + 2(2) = 5$

$x + 4 = 5$

$x = 5 - 4$

$x = 1$

Solve the following pair of simultaneous equations:

$$2p - 3q = 9 \quad \text{and} \quad 5p + 2q = 13.$$

key point

Sometimes it is necessary to multiply both rows by a number to get a variable to cancel.

Solution

To eliminate the q's:

Step 1: ① $2p - 3q = 9$ $\quad (\times 2)$

 ② $\underline{5p + 2q = 13}$ $\quad (\times 3)$

Step 2: ① $4p - 6q = 18$

 ② $\underline{15p + 6q = 39}$ (add the rows)

Step 3: $\qquad 19p = 57$ $\quad (\div 19)$

Step 4: $\qquad p = 3$

Therefore, the solution is $p = 3$, $q = -1$.

To find the value for q, let $p = 3$ in either of the equations:

Step 5: ② $5p + 2q = 13$

$5(3) + 2q = 13$

$15 + 2q = 13$

$2q = 13 - 15$

$2q = -2$

$q = -1$

(i) Solve the simultaneous equations $x + 2y = 4$ and $x - y = 1$.

(ii) By graphing the two lines on a single co-ordinate diagram, check your answer to part **(i)**.

Solution

(i) Solve the simultaneous equations:

Step 1: ① $x + 2y = 4$

      ② $\underline{x - y = 1}$ (× 2)

Step 2: ① $x + 2y = 4$

      ② $\underline{2x - 2y = 2}$

Step 3: $3x = 6$ (÷3)

Step 4: $x = 2$

Therefore, the solution is $x = 2$, $y = 1$.

To find the value for y, let $x = 2$ in either of the equations:

Step 5: ① $x + 2y = 4$

         $2 + 2y = 4$

         $2y = 4 - 2$

         $2y = 2$

         $y = 1$

(ii) To graph the lines, we need to find the points where they cross the x- and y-axes.

The process of graphing lines is covered in detail in the chapter on graphing functions and also the chapter on Coordinate Geometry of the Line in the *Less Stress More Success* book for Paper 2.

For $x + 2y = 4$:

On the x-axis, $y = 0$:

       $x + 2(0) = 4$

            $x = 4$

Line crosses x-axis at $(4, 0)$.

On the y-axis, $x = 0$:

       $0 + 2y = 4$

            $2y = 4$

             $y = 2$

Line crosses y-axis at $(0, 2)$.

For $x - y = 1$:

On the x-axis, $y = 0$:

       $x - 0 = 1$

           $x = 1$

Line crosses x-axis at $(1, 0)$.

On the y-axis, $x = 0$:

       $0 - y = 1$

          $-y = 1$

           $y = -1$

Line crosses y-axis at $(0, -1)$.

Graphing the lines:

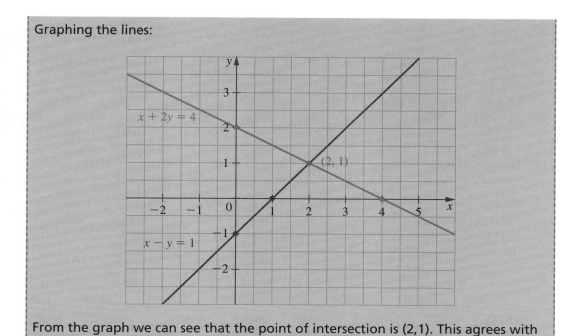

$x + 2y = 4$

$x - y = 1$

$(2, 1)$

From the graph we can see that the point of intersection is (2,1). This agrees with the answer from part **(i)**.

Using simultaneous equations in real-world scenarios

Read the given information carefully and use it to form two equations. Then solve these equations simultaneously.

Suzanne is saving for Christmas. Throughout the year she collects savings stamps at the post office. By December she has €25 saved. This is made up of 20 cent saving stamps and 50 cent saving stamps. She has 104 saving stamps in total. Let x be the number of 20 cent saving stamps and y be the number of 50 cent saving stamps.

(i) Write an equation in x and y to represent the total number of stamps Suzanne has.

(ii) Write an equation in x and y to represent the total value of Suzanne's stamps.

(iii) Solve the equations to find the number of each type of stamp Suzanne has.

Solution

x = number of 20c stamps

y = number of 50c stamps

(i) Total number of stamps = $x + y$

$$104 = x + y$$

(ii) Value of stamps in cent = $20(x) + 50(y)$

$$2,500 = 20x + 50y$$

$$250 = 2x + 5y$$

key point

Be aware that values were given here in both euro and cent. You must change to the same units before you begin the question.

(iii) Solve the equations:

Step 1: ① $\quad x + y = 104 \qquad (\times -2)$

② $\quad \underline{2x + 5y = 250}$

Step 2: ① $\quad -2x - 2y = -208$

② $\quad \underline{2x + 5y = 250}$

Step 3: $\qquad\qquad 3y = 42$

Step 4: $\qquad\qquad\quad y = 14$

Let $y = 14$:

Step 5: ① $\quad x + y = 104$

$\qquad\qquad x + 14 = 104$

$\qquad\qquad\qquad x = 90$

Therefore, Suzanne has ninety 20c saving stamps and fourteen 50c saving stamps.

Example

Let the cost of a meal for an adult be €x and the cost of a meal for a child be €y. The cost of a meal for 3 adults and 2 children amounts to €125. The cost of a meal for 2 adults and 3 children amounts to €115.

(i) Write an equation in x and y to represent the cost of a meal for 3 adults and 2 children.

(ii) Write an equation in x and y to represent the cost of a meal for 2 adults and 3 children.

(iii) Solve these equations to find the cost of an adult's meal and the cost of a child's meal.

Solution

(i) The cost of a meal for 3 adults and 2 children amounts to €125: $3x + 2y = 125$.

(ii) The cost of a meal for 2 adults and 3 children amounts to €115: $2x + 3y = 115$.

(iii) Solving simultaneously:

Step 1: ① $3x + 2y = 125$ $(\times -3)$

      ② $2x + 3y = 115$ $(\times 2)$

Step 2: ① $-9x - 6y = -375$

      ② $4x + 6y = 230$

Step 3: $-5x \quad\quad = -145$ $(\div -5)$

Step 4: $x = 29$

Substitute $x = 29$ into one of the equations:

Step 5:

① $3(29) + 2y = 125$

     $87 + 2y = 125$

         $2y = 125 - 87$

         $2y = 38$

          $y = 19$

Therefore, an adult meal costs €29 and a child's meal costs €19.

The cost of five books and one magazine is €32.

The cost of eight books and three magazines is €54.

Let €*b* be the cost of a book and let €*m* be the cost of a magazine.

(i) Write an equation in *b* and *m* to represent the cost of five books and one magazine.

(ii) Write an equation in *b* and *m* to represent the cost of eight books and three magazines.

(iii) Solve the equations to find the cost of a book and the cost of a magazine.

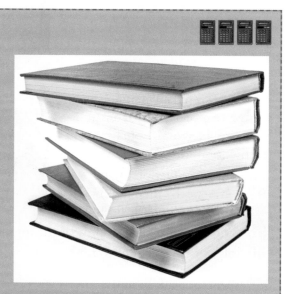

Solution

(i) Five books + one magazine = 32

$$5b + m = 32$$

(ii) Eight books and three magazines = 54

$$8b + 3m = 54$$

(iii) Solve the equations:

Step 1: ① $5b + m = 32$ $(\times -3)$

② $8b + 3m = 54$

Step 2: ① $-15b - 3m = -96$

② $8b + 3m = 54$

Step 3: $-7b = -42$ $(\div -7)$

Step 4: $b = 6$

Let $b = 6$:

Step 5: ① $5b + m = 32$

$5(6) + m = 32$

$30 + m = 32$

$m = 32 - 30$

$m = 2$

Therefore, a book costs €6 and a magazine costs €2.

Example

An examination paper consists of 40 questions.

5 marks are given for each correct answer.

3 marks are deducted for each incorrect answer.

Kenny answered all 40 questions, getting x correct and getting y incorrect. His total score for the examination was 56 marks.

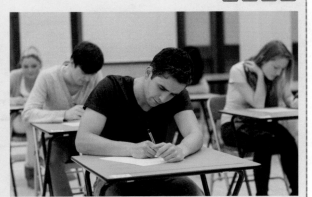

(i) Write an equation to represent the total number of questions Kenny answered.

(ii) Write an equation to represent the total number of marks Kenny scored.

(iii) Solve these equations to find how many questions Kenny answered correctly.

Solution

(i) Total number of questions $= x + y$

$$40 = x + y$$

(ii) Total marks $= 5(x) + (-3)(y)$

$$56 = 5x - 3y$$

(iii) Solve the equations:

Step 1: ① $x + y = 40$ $\quad(\times 3)$ Let $x = 22$:

        ② $5x - 3y = 56$ **Step 5:** ① $x + y = 40$

Step 2: ① $3x + 3y = 120$ $22 + y = 40$

        ② $5x - 3y = 56$ $y = 40 - 22$

Step 3: $\quad\quad\quad\quad 8x = 176$ $y = 18$

Step 4: $\quad\quad\quad\quad x = 22$

Therefore, Kenny answered 22 questions correctly and 18 questions incorrectly.

John and Gemma played a new computer game called Benga.
John scored two bengas minus three penalties. His score was
seven points. He made the equation $2x - 3y = 7$ to represent his score.
Gemma scored five bengas minus five penalties for 20 points.

 (i) Make an equation to represent Gemma's score.

 (ii) Use simultaneous equations to find the number of points for a benga and the
    number of points for a penalty.

(iii) Verify your solutions in both equations.

Solution

 (i) Five bengas minus five penalties for 20 points:
    $5x - 5y = 20$

(ii) Solve the equations:

Step 1: ① $\quad 2x - 3y = 7$ $\quad(\times 5)$ Let $x = 5$:

        ② $\quad 5x - 5y = 20$ $\quad(\times -3)$ **Step 5:** ① $\quad 2x - 3y = 7$

Step 2: ① $\quad 10x - 15y = 35$ $2(5) - 3y = 7$

        ② $-15x + 15y = -60$ $10 - 3y = 7$

Step 3: $\quad\quad\quad -5x = -25$ $\quad(\div -5)$ $-3y = 7 - 10$

Step 4: $\quad\quad\quad\quad\quad x = 5$ $-3y = -3$ $\quad(\div -3)$

                                            $y = 1$

Therefore, a benga is worth 5 points and a penalty is worth 1 point.

(iii) John: $2x - 3y = 7$ Gemma: $5x - 5y = 20$

        $2(5) - 3(1) = 7$ $5(5) - 5(1) = 20$

          $10 - 3 = 7$ $25 - 5 = 20$

            $7 = 7$ $20 = 20$

Equations are balanced in each case, thus we have verified the solutions.

This question was very badly answered and subsequently the **entire** question was worth 5 marks.

4 marks were awarded for getting any two out of the three parts correct.

3 marks were awarded for getting any one of the three parts correct.

No marks awarded for blanks! Make sure to attempt all parts of every question.

7 Long Division in Algebra

aims

☐ To learn how to divide algebraic expressions into one another.
☐ To be able to use long division in algebra, where necessary, in solving in-context questions.

Division in algebra follows the same procedure as division in arithmetic. Divide the numbers into the numbers and the algebraic parts into the algebraic parts.

The stages in dividing one algebraic expression by another are shown in the following example.

Example

Simplify.

(i) $\dfrac{-2x}{x}$ (ii) $\dfrac{24b}{8b}$ (iii) $\dfrac{-6p^2}{3p}$ (iv) $\dfrac{10a^2}{2a}$

Solution

(i) $\dfrac{-2x}{x} = \dfrac{(-2)(x)}{(1)(x)} = (-2)(1) = -2$

(-2 divided by 1 is -2.
x divided by x is 1.)

(ii) $\dfrac{24b}{8b} = \dfrac{(24)(b)}{(8)(b)} = (3)(1) = 3$

(24 divided by 8 is 3.
b divided by b is 1.)

(iii) $\dfrac{-6p^2}{3p} = \dfrac{(-6)(p)(p)}{(3)(p)} = (-2)(1)(p) = -2p$

(-6 divided by 3 is -2.
p^2 divided by p is p.)

(iv) $\dfrac{10a^2}{2a} = \dfrac{(10)(a)(a)}{(2)(a)} = (5)(1)(a) = 5a$

(10 divided by 2 is 5.
a^2 divided by a is a.)

key point

Divide the number on the top by the number on the bottom.
Divide the algebraic part on the top by the algebraic part on the bottom.

Dividing a quadratic expression by a linear expression

There are two methods for dividing a linear expression into a quadratic expression:

Method 1: Put the quadratic over the linear.

Factorise the quadratic.

Divide top and bottom by the linear expression.

Method 2: Follow the same procedure as long division in arithmetic.

The steps for this method are shown in the following example.

Example

Divide $x^2 + x - 12$ by $x + 4$.

Solution

Method 1: $\dfrac{x^2 + x - 12}{x + 4}$ (place the $x^2 + x - 12$ over the $x + 4$)

$\dfrac{(x + 4)(x - 3)}{x + 4}$ (factorise the top)

$\dfrac{\cancel{(x + 4)}(x - 3)}{\cancel{x + 4}}$ (divide top and bottom by $(x + 4)$)

$x - 3$

Method 2:

$$
\begin{array}{r}
x - 3 \\
x + 4 \enclose{longdiv}{x^2 + x - 12} \\
\end{array}
$$

$x^2 + 4x \downarrow$ ($x^2 \div x = x$, put x on top)

$-3x - 12$ (multiply $x(x + 4) = x^2 + 4x$)

(subtract bottom row from top and bring down -12)

($-3x \div x = -3$, put -3 on top)

$-3x - 12$ (multiply $-3(x + 4) = -3x - 12$)

0 (subtract bottom row from the top)

Therefore, $(x^2 + x - 12) \div (x + 4) = x - 3$.

Notice the importance of factorising here. Factorising is an important skill for you to have throughout your course.

Divide $x^2 - 3x - 10$ by $x + 2$.

Solution

Method 1: $\dfrac{x^2 - 3x - 10}{x + 2}$ (place the $x^2 - 3x - 10$ over the $x + 2$)

$\dfrac{(x + 2)(x - 5)}{x + 2}$ (factorise the top)

$x - 5$ (divide top and bottom by $x + 2$)

Method 2:

$$
\begin{array}{r}
x - 5 \\
x + 2 \,\overline{\smash{)}\, x^2 - 3x - 10} \\
\underline{x^2 + 2x} \quad\downarrow \\
-5x - 10 \\
\underline{-5x - 10} \\
0
\end{array}
$$

($x^2 \div x = x$, put x on top)

(multiply $x(x + 2) = x^2 + 2x$)

(subtract bottom row from top and bring down -10)
($-5x \div x = -5$, put -5 on top)
($-5(x + 2) = -5x - 10$)

(subtract bottom row from the top row)

Therefore, $(x^2 - 3x - 10) \div (x + 2) = x - 5$.

Example

Divide $5x^2 + 13x + 6$ by $5x + 3$.

Solution

$$
\begin{array}{r}
x + 2 \\
5x + 3 \,\overline{\smash{)}\, 5x^2 + 13x + 6} \\
\underline{5x^2 + 3x} \quad\downarrow \\
10x + 6 \\
\underline{10x + 6} \\
0
\end{array}
$$

($5x^2 \div 5x = x$, put x on top)

(multiply $x(5x + 3) = 5x^2 + 3x$)

(subtract bottom row from top and bring down $+6$)
($10x \div 5x = 2$, put 2 on top)

(multiply $2(5x + 3) = 10x + 6$)

(subtract bottom row from the top)

Therefore, $(5x^2 + 13x + 6) \div (5x + 3) = x + 2$.

Divide $6x^2 - x - 2$ by $3x - 2$.

Solution

$$
\begin{array}{r}
2x + 1 \\
3x - 2 \overline{\smash{\big)}\ 6x^2 - x - 2} \\
\end{array}
$$

$$6x^2 - 4x \quad \downarrow$$

$$3x - 2$$

$$3x - 2$$

$$0$$

$\qquad$ ($6x^2 \div 3x = 2x$, put $2x$ on top)

$\qquad$ (multiply $2x(3x - 2) = 6x^2 - 4x$)

$\qquad$ (subtract bottom row from the top and bring down -2)

$\qquad$ ($3x \div 3x = 1$, put 1 on top)

$\qquad$ (multiply $1(3x - 2) = 3x - 2$)

$\qquad$ (subtract bottom row from the top)

Therefore, $(6x^2 - x - 2) \div (3x - 2) = 2x + 1$.

The diagram shows a rectangular box.
It has a width of $2x - 1$.

Given that the area of the rectangle is
$8x^2 + 6x - 5$, find the length of the
rectangle.

Length

Width $= 2x - 1$

Solution

Area of a box $=$ (Length)(Width)

$$\frac{\text{Area of box}}{\text{Width}} = \text{Length} \quad \rightarrow \quad \frac{8x^2 + 6x - 5}{2x - 1} = \text{Length}$$

Division:

$$
\begin{array}{r}
4x + 5 \\
2x - 1 \overline{\smash{\big)}\ 8x^2 + 6x - 5} \\
\end{array}
$$

$$8x^2 - 4x \quad \downarrow$$

$$10x - 5$$

$$10x - 5$$

$$0$$

$\qquad$ ($8x^2 \div 2x = 4x$, put $4x$ on top)

$\qquad$ (multiply $4x(2x - 1) = 8x^2 - 4x$)

$\qquad$ (subtract bottom row from top and bring down -5)

$\qquad$ ($10x \div 2x = 5$, put 5 on top)

$\qquad$ (subtract bottom row from top)

Therefore, length of the rectangle $= 4x + 5$.

8 Inequalities

☐ To learn how to solve linear inequalities.

☐ To learn how to graph a solution set on a number line.

☐ To be able to apply inequality methods to in-context questions.

The four inequality symbols are:

1. $>$ means greater than
2. $\geq$ means greater than or equal to
3. $<$ means less than
4. $\leq$ means less than or equal to

Algebraic expressions that are linked by one of the four inequality symbols are called **inequalities**. For example, $3x - 1 \geq 11$ and $-3 < 2x - 1 \leq 7$ are inequalities.

Solving inequalities is exactly the same as solving equations, with the following exception:

Multiplying or dividing both sides of an inequality by a negative number reverses the direction of the inequality symbol.

That is:

$>$ changes to $<$ $\geq$ changes to $\leq$

$<$ changes to $>$ $\leq$ changes to $\geq$

Solving an inequality means finding the values of x that make the inequality true.

The following rules apply to graphing inequalities on a number line:

Number line for $x \in \mathbb{N}$ or $x \in \mathbb{Z}$, use dots.

Number line for $x \in \mathbb{R}$, use a full heavy line.

Note: Inequalities can be turned around. For example:

$5 \leq x$ means the same as $x \geq 5$.

$8 \geq x \geq 3$ means the same as $3 \leq x \leq 8$.

Example

Graph on the number line the solution set of $2x + 1 < 9$, $x \in \mathbb{N}$.

Solution

$$2x + 1 < 9$$
$$2x + 1 - 1 < 9 - 1 \qquad \text{(subtract 1 from both sides)}$$
$$2x < 8 \qquad \text{(simplify)}$$
$$x < 4 \qquad \text{(divide both sides by 2)}$$

As $x \in \mathbb{N}$, this is the set of natural numbers less than 4.

Thus, the values of x are 1, 2 and 3.

Number line:

Note: As $x \in \mathbb{N}$, dots are used on the number line.

Example

Graph on the number line the solution set of $3x - 4 \geq 8$, $x \in \mathbb{Z}$.

Solution

$$3x - 4 \geq 8$$
$$3x - 4 + 4 \geq 8 + 4 \qquad \text{(add 4 to both sides)}$$
$$3x \geq 12 \qquad \text{(simplify)}$$
$$x \geq 4 \qquad \text{(divide both sides by 3)}$$

As $x \in \mathbb{Z}$, this is the set of natural numbers greater than or equal to 4.

Thus, the values of x are 4, 5, 6, 7, $\dots$

Number line:

Note: As $x \in \mathbb{Z}$, dots are used on the number line.

Students often have difficulty determining the correct region for the final answer. Spend some time practising this.

Example

Graph on the number line the solution set of $3x - 5 \leq x + 7$, $x \in \mathbb{Z}$.

Solution

$$3x - 5 \leq x + 7$$
$3x - 5 - x \leq x + 7 - x$ (subtract x from both sides)
$2x - 5 + 5 \leq 7 + 5$ (add 5 to both sides)
$\qquad 2x \leq 12$ (simplify)
$\qquad x \leq 6$ (divide both sides by 2)

As $x \in \mathbb{Z}$, this is the set of integers (whole numbers) less than or equal to 6.
Thus, the values of x are $6, 5, 4, 3, 2, 1, 0, -1, -2, \ldots$

Number line:

Note: As $x \in \mathbb{Z}$, dots are used on the number line.

Example

Graph on the number line the solution set of $4x - 1 \geq 2x + 5$, $x \in \mathbb{R}$.

Solution

$$4x - 1 \geq 2x + 5$$
$4x - 1 + 1 \geq 2x + 5 + 1$ (add 1 to both sides)
$4x - 2x \geq 2x + 6 - 2x$ (subtract $2x$ from both sides)
$\qquad 2x \geq 6$ (simplify)
$\qquad x \geq 3$ (divide both sides by 2)

As $x \in \mathbb{R}$, this is the set of real numbers greater than or equal to 3.
Number line:

Note: 1. As $x \in \mathbb{R}$, we use full heavy shading on the number line.
     2. A dot is put on 3 to indicate that it is included in the solution.

Find the values of x for which $4x - 1 < 11$, $x \in \mathbb{N}$.

Solution
$$4x - 1 < 11$$
$$4x - 1 + 1 < 11 + 1 \qquad \text{(add 1 to both sides)}$$
$$4x < 12$$
$$x < 3 \qquad \text{(divide both sides by 3)}$$

Since $x \in \mathbb{N}$, x is a positive whole number, which must be less than 3.
Therefore, $x = 1$ or 2.

Example

Graph on the number line the solution set of $2x - 1 > 9$, $x \in \mathbb{Z}$.

Solution

$$2x - 1 > 9$$
$$2x > 9 + 1 \qquad \text{(add 1 to both sides)}$$
$$2x > 10 \qquad \text{(simplify)}$$
$$x > 5 \qquad \text{(divide both sides by 2)}$$

As $x \in \mathbb{Z}$, this is the set of integers (whole numbers) greater than 5.
Thus, the values of x are 6, 7, 8, 9, 10, etc.
Number line:

Note: As $x \in \mathbb{Z}$, dots are used on the number line.

Find the largest possible value of n such that $5n + 48 > 8n - 6$, $n \in \mathbb{N}$.

Solution

$$5n + 48 > 8n - 6$$

$$5n + 48 + 6 > 8n - 6 + 6 \qquad \text{(add 6 to both sides)}$$

$$5n + 54 > 8n$$

$$5n - 5n + 54 > 8n - 5n \qquad \text{(subtract } 5n \text{ from both sides)}$$

$$54 > 3n \qquad \text{(divide both sides by 3)}$$

$$18 > n$$

Rearrange to get: $n < 18$.

Since $n \in \mathbb{N}$, n is a positive whole number.

The largest positive whole number less than 18 is 17.

Therefore, the largest value of n is 17.

key point

$18 > n$ means the same as $n < 18$. Read the inequality from the variable 'n is less than 18.'

Find the range of values of $x \in \mathbb{R}$ for which $4(x - 2) > 5(2x - 1) - 9$ and graph your solution on the number line.

Solution

$$4(x - 2) > 5(2x - 1) - 9$$

$$4x - 8 > 10x - 5 - 9 \qquad \text{(remove the brackets)}$$

$$4x - 8 > 10x - 14 \qquad \text{(simplify)}$$

$$4x - 8 + 14 - 4x > 10x - 14 + 14 - 4x \qquad \text{(subtract } 4x \text{ and add 14 to both sides)}$$

$$6 > 6x \qquad \text{(simplify)}$$

$$1 > x \qquad \text{(divide both sides by 6)}$$

Reading from the x: $x < 1$.

Number line:

Note: 1. As $x \in \mathbb{R}$, we use full heavy shading on the number line.

2. A hollow circle is put around 1 to indicate that it is **not** included in the solution.

key point

The inequality is $<$ and not $\leq$, so you must put a circle on the number line and not a dot.

Example

(i) Find the solution set P of $3x + 8 \leq 14, x \in \mathbb{R}$.

(ii) Find the solution set Q of $5 - 2x < 11, x \in \mathbb{R}$.

(iii) Find $P \cap Q$ and graph your solution on the number line.

Solution

We solve each inequality separately and then combine the solutions.

(i) P: $3x + 8 \leq 14$

$3x \leq 6$

$x \leq 2$

(ii) Q: $5 - 2x < 11$

$5 - 11 < 2x$

$-6 < 2x$

$-3 < x$

So $x > -3$.

(iii) Combining the two inequalities gives:

$P \cap Q$: $-3 < x \leq 2$, $x \in \mathbb{R}$

This is the set of positive and negative real numbers between -3 and 2, including 2 but not including -3.

Number line:

We were not asked to draw the number lines in parts (i) and (ii), but as you can see from below, these number lines are helpful when plotting the final solution set:

(i) P: $x \leq 2$

(ii) Q: $x > -3$

$P \cap Q$: $-3 < x \leq 2$

Note: 1. As $x \in \mathbb{R}$, we use full heavy shading on the number line.

2. A hollow circle is put around -3 to indicate that it is **not** included in the solution.

3. A dot is put on 2 to indicate that it **is** included in the solution.

(i) Find A, the solution set of $3x - 5 < 7, x \in \mathbb{Z}$.

(ii) Find B, the solution set of $-2 - 3x \leq 4, x \in \mathbb{Z}$.

(iii) List the elements of $A \cap B$.

Solution

(i) $3x - 5 < 7$

$\quad\quad 3x < 7 + 5$ (add 5 to both sides)

$\quad\quad 3x < 12$

$\quad\quad\quad x < 4$ (divide both sides by 3)

Therefore, set A contains all integers less than 4.

$A = \{3, 2, 1, 0, -1, -2, -3, -4, \ldots\}$

(ii) $\quad\quad\quad\quad -2 - 3x \leq 4$

$\quad -2 - 3x - 4 + 3x \leq 4 - 4 + 3x$ (subtract 4 and add $3x$ to both sides)

$\quad\quad\quad\quad\quad -6 \leq 3x$ (simplify)

$\quad\quad\quad\quad\quad -2 \leq x$ (divide both sides by 3)

Therefore, set B contains all integers greater than or equal to -2.

$B = \{-2, -1, 0, 1, 2, 3, 4, 5, 6, \ldots\}$

(iii) To find $A \cap B$ we must combine the two inequalities: $A \cap B = -2 \leq x < 4$.

Therefore, the elements of $A \cap B$ are $\{-2, -1, 0, 1, 2, 3\}$.

Notice that the question just asked for a list of the answers and not a number line.

In-context questions

The following questions involve the use of inequalities in real-world situations.

The width of a rectangle is x cm and its length is $(2x - 3)$cm, where $x \in \mathbb{N}$.

(i) Find an expression, in terms of x, for the perimeter of the rectangle.

(ii) If the perimeter of the rectangle must be greater than 42cm, find the smallest possible value of x.

(iii) Hence, find the area of the rectangle for this value of x.

x cm

$(2x - 3)$cm

Solution

(i) Perimeter = 2(Length) + 2(Width)

$$= 2(2x - 3) + 2(x)$$
$$= 4x - 6 + 2x$$
$$= 6x - 6$$

(ii) Perimeter > 42

$$6x - 6 > 42 \qquad \text{(from (i))}$$
$$6x > 48$$
$$x > 8\text{cm}$$

Therefore, the smallest possible value of x is 9cm, since $x \in \mathbb{N}$.

(iii) If $x = 9$:

Width = 9　　and　　Length = 2(9) − 3 = 15

Area = Length × Width

$$= 9 \times 15$$
$$= 135\text{cm}^2$$

Sharon called A1 Towing to tow her car after it broke down. A1 Towing charges a €75·00 call-out fee and €3·00 per kilometre after the first 10 kilometres towed.

Let k be the number of kilometres towed over 10km.

(i) Find the cost of getting a car towed 15 kilometres with this towing company.

(ii) Write an expression for the cost of getting a car towed a distance of k kilometres beyond the first 10 kilometres with this towing company.

(iii) Sharon can afford to spend no more than €115 towing her car. Write an inequality in terms of k to represent this information.

(iv) Solve the inequality from (iii) and hence find the total maximum number of whole kilometres Sharon can get her car towed.

Solution

(i) Cost of towing 15km = (€75 call-out charge) + (€3 per km over 10km)

$$= (€75) + (€3 × 5km)$$
$$= €75 + €15$$
$$= €90$$

(ii) Let k = number of km travelled beyond 10 km.

Cost of towing = (€75 call-out charge) + (€3 per km over 10km)

$$= (€75) + (€3 × k)$$
$$= €75 + €3(k)$$

(iii) Cost of towing ≤ €115

$$€75 + €3(k) ≤ €115$$
$$75 + 3k ≤ 115$$

(iv) $75 + 3k ≤ 115$

$$3k ≤ 115 − 75$$
$$3k ≤ 40$$
$$k ≤ 13·33333$$

Therefore, Sharon can get her car towed 13km beyond the 10km, so she can get her car towed a total distance of 23 km.

9 Indices

In the expression a^m, a is the base and m is the index.

The index can also be called the power or the exponent.

key
point

a^m is read as 'a to the power of m'.

Example

Using the calculator or otherwise, evaluate:

(i) 8^4 (ii) 12^3 (iii) 3^6

Solution

(i) $8^4 = 8 \times 8 \times 8 \times 8 = 4{,}096$

(ii) $12^3 = 12 \times 12 \times 12 = 1{,}728$

(iii) $3^6 = 3 \times 3 \times 3 \times 3 \times 3 \times 3 = 729$

key
point

If the power is very large, it is quicker and easier to use the power button on the calculator: $\boxed{x^\blacksquare}$ or $\boxed{y^\blacksquare}$

Example: 6^9 can be entered as $\boxed{6}$ $\boxed{x^\blacksquare}$ $\boxed{9}$ $\boxed{=}$ 10077696

The table below shows the values when 2 is raised to certain powers.

(i) Complete the table.

Power of 2	Expanded power of 2	Answer
2^1	2	2
2^2	2 × 2	4
2^3	2 × 2 × 2	
2^4		
2^5		
2^6		
2^7		
2^8		
2^9		

(ii) Maria wins a prize in a lottery and is given two options.

Option A: €1,000 cash today

Option B: Take €2 today, €4 tomorrow, €8 the next day and doubling every day for 9 days.

Which option should Maria choose if she wants to get the most prize money? Explain your answer.

Solution

(i) Completed table:

Power of 2	Expanded power of 2	Answer
2^1	2	2
2^2	2 × 2	4
2^3	2 × 2 × 2	8
2^4	2 × 2 × 2 × 2	16
2^5	2 × 2 × 2 × 2 × 2	32
2^6	2 × 2 × 2 × 2 × 2 × 2	64
2^7	2 × 2 × 2 × 2 × 2 × 2 × 2	128
2^8	2 × 2 × 2 × 2 × 2 × 2 × 2 × 2	256
2^9	2 × 2 × 2 × 2 × 2 × 2 × 2 × 2 × 2	512

(ii) Option A: €1,000 now

Option B: €2 + €4 + €8 + €16 + €32 + €64 + €128 + €256 + €512 = €1,022

Maria should choose option B because it will give her €22 more than option A.

Rules of Indices		
Where $a \in \mathbb{R}$; $p, q \in \mathbb{Q}$; $a \neq 0$:		
Rules (see booklet of formulae and tables).	**Example**	
1. $a^p a^q = a^{p+q}$	$5^4 5^3 = 5^{4+3} = 5^7$	$x^3 x^5 = x^{3+5} = x^8$
2. $\dfrac{a^p}{a^q} = a^{p-q}$	$\dfrac{3^5}{3^2} = 3^{5-2} = 3^3$	$\dfrac{x^7}{x^3} = x^{7-3} = x^4$
3. $(a^p)^q = a^{pq}$	$(3^2)^4 = 3^8$	$(x^3)^4 = x^{12}$

Example

(i) Write $a^4 \times a^3$ in the form a^n, where $n \in \mathbb{N}$.

(ii) Hence or otherwise, evaluate $2^4 \times 2^3$.

Solution

(i) $a^4 \times a^3 = a^{4+3} = a^7$ (use rule: $a^p a^q = a^{p+q}$)

(ii) $2^4 \times 2^3 = 2^7 = 128$ (use calculator to evaluate 2^7)

Example

(i) Write $\dfrac{p^7}{p^3}$ in the form p^n, where $n \in \mathbb{N}$.

(ii) Hence or otherwise, evaluate $\dfrac{11^7}{11^3}$.

Solution

(i) $\dfrac{p^7}{p^3} = p^{7-3} = p^4$ (use rule: $\dfrac{a^p}{a^q} = a^{p-q}$)

(ii) $\dfrac{11^7}{11^3} = 11^4 = 14{,}641$ (use calculator to evaluate 11^4)

Example

(i) Write $(r^3)^2$ in the form r^n, where $n \in \mathbb{N}$.

(ii) Hence or otherwise, evaluate $(5^3)^2$.

Solution

(i) $(r^3)^2 = r^{3 \times 2} = r^6$ (use rule: $(a^p)^q = a^{pq}$)

(ii) $(5^3)^2 = 5^6 = 15,625$ (use calculator to evaluate 5^6)

Find the exact value of $(4^2)^3$.

Solution

Method 1: Using rules of indices: $(4^2)^3$

$4^{2 \times 3}$ (use rule: $(a^p)^q = a^{pq}$)

4^6 (simplify)

$4,096$ (use calculator to evaluate 4^6)

Method 2: Using the calculator: $(4^2)^3$

$(16)^3$ (use calculator to evaluate 4^2)

$4,096$ (use calculator to evaluate 16^3)

Simplify $(a^3 \times a \times a^4)^2$.

Solution

$(a^3 \times a \times a^4)^2$

$(a^3 \times a^1 \times a^4)^2$

$(a^{3+1+4})^2$ (use rule: $a^p a^q = a^{p+q}$)

$(a^8)^2$ (simplify)

$a^{8 \times 2}$ (use rule: $(a^p)^q = a^{pq}$)

a^{16}

Example

Evaluate $36^{\frac{1}{2}}$.

Solution

Using the calculator: $36^{\frac{1}{2}} = 6$.

A special index: $a^{\frac{1}{2}} = \sqrt{a}$

Example: $16^{\frac{1}{2}} = \sqrt{16} = 4$

Example

Evaluate $25^{\frac{1}{2}}$.

Solution

$25^{\frac{1}{2}} = \sqrt{25} = 5$

Using a calculator or otherwise, find the exact value of:

(i) $(2 \cdot 25)^{\frac{1}{2}}$ **(ii)** $(3 \cdot 61)^{\frac{1}{2}}$

Solution

(i) $(2 \cdot 25)^{\frac{1}{2}} = \sqrt{2 \cdot 25} = 1 \cdot 5$ (use calculator to evaluate $\sqrt{2 \cdot 25}$)

(ii) $(3 \cdot 61)^{\frac{1}{2}} = \sqrt{3 \cdot 61} = 1 \cdot 9$ (use calculator to evaluate $\sqrt{3 \cdot 61}$)

Example

Simplify $\dfrac{a^9 \times a^3}{a^6 \times a^2}$. Give your answer in the form a^n, where $n \in \mathbb{N}$.

Solution

$\dfrac{a^9 \times a^3}{a^6 \times a^2}$

$\dfrac{a^{9+3}}{a^{6+2}}$ (use rule: $a^p a^q = a^{p+q}$)

$\dfrac{a^{12}}{a^8}$ (simplify the powers)

a^{12-8} (use rule: $\dfrac{a^p}{a^q} = a^{p-q}$)

a^4 (simplify the powers)

(i) Simplify $\dfrac{b^5 \times b^2}{b \times b^3}$. Give your answer in the form b^n, where $n \in \mathbb{N}$.

(ii) Using your answer to part **(i)**, or otherwise, find the value of $\dfrac{6^5 \times 6^2}{6 \times 6^3}$.

Solution

(i) $\dfrac{b^5 \times b^2}{b \times b^3}$ $(b = b^1)$

$\dfrac{b^{5+2}}{b^{1+3}}$ (use rule: $a^p a^q = a^{p+q}$)

$\dfrac{b^7}{b^4}$ (simplify the powers)

b^{7-4} (use rule: $\dfrac{a^p}{a^q} = a^{p-q}$)

b^3 (simplify the powers)

(ii) $\dfrac{6^5 \times 6^2}{6 \times 6^3} = 6^3$ (from part **(i)**, replacing b with 6)

        $= 216$

Reciprocals

If the product of two numbers is 1, then each number is the reciprocal of the other.

The reciprocal of 5 is $\dfrac{1}{5}$ and the reciprocal of $\dfrac{1}{5}$ is 5.

> Examples of reciprocals:
>
> $5 \times \dfrac{1}{5} = 1$ $\dfrac{2}{3} \times \dfrac{3}{2} = 1$ $-\dfrac{7}{9} \times -\dfrac{9}{7} = 1$

To find the reciprocal of a number, do the following.

Method 1: Write the given number as a single fraction and turn it upside down.
Method 2: Use the reciprocal button, $\boxed{x^{-1}}$ or $\boxed{1/x}$, on your calculator.

Example

(i) Write down the reciprocal of 9.

(ii) Find the value of this reciprocal, correct to two decimal places.

Solution

(i) **Method 1:** Reciprocal of $9 = \dfrac{1}{9}$

Method 2: Reciprocal of $9 = (9)^{-1} = \dfrac{1}{9}$

(ii) $\dfrac{1}{9} = 0{\cdot}1111111 = 0{\cdot}11$ (correct to two decimal places)

Write the reciprocal of 10,000.

Solution

Reciprocal of $10{,}000 = \dfrac{1}{10{,}000} = 0{\cdot}0001$

Example

(i) Write down the reciprocal of $\dfrac{7}{2}$.

(ii) Find the value of this reciprocal, correct to two decimal places.

Solution

(i) **Method 1:** Reciprocal of $\dfrac{7}{2} = \dfrac{2}{7}$

Method 2: Reciprocal of $\dfrac{7}{2} = \left(\dfrac{7}{2}\right)^{-1} = \dfrac{2}{7}$

(ii) $\dfrac{2}{7} = 0{\cdot}285714 = 0{\cdot}29$ (correct to two decimal places)

Using a calculator or otherwise, find the exact value of:

(i) $(4 \cdot 6)^2$ **(ii)** $9^{\frac{1}{2}}$ **(iii)** $\dfrac{1}{6 \cdot 4}$

Solution

(i) $(4 \cdot 6)^2 = 21 \cdot 16$ (using calculator)

(ii) Method 1: $9^{\frac{1}{2}} = 3$ (using calculator)

      Method 2: $9^{\frac{1}{2}} = \sqrt{9} = 3$ (using rule $a^{\frac{1}{2}} = \sqrt{a}$)

(iii) Method 1: $\dfrac{1}{6 \cdot 4} = 0 \cdot 15625$ (using calculator)

      Method 2: $\dfrac{1}{6 \cdot 4} = (6 \cdot 4)^{-1} = 0 \cdot 15625$ (using reciprocal button on calculator)

10 Pattern

- ☐ To recognise a repeating pattern and to make predictions from that pattern.
- ☐ To represent patterns with tables, diagrams and graphs.
- ☐ To generate and write expressions and formulae from patterns for particular terms in a sequence.
- ☐ To know about linear, quadratic and exponential patterns.
- ☐ To understand and be able to carry out the operation called differencing.

An introduction to pattern

A pattern always has a logical sequence.

Examples of pattern in everyday life:

  1. Traffic lights: Green, Amber, Red, Green, Amber, . . .
  2. Weekdays: M, T, W, T, F, M, T, W, . . .
  3. Tidal movements: High tide, Low tide, High tide, Low tide, . . .
  4. Notes of the scale: doh, ray, me, fah, doh, ray, . . .

Sequences

A sequence is a particular order in which related things follow each other. For example:

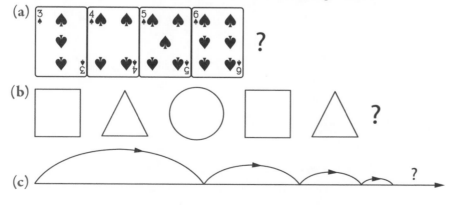

(a)

(b)

(c)

(d) 1, 3, 6, 10, **?**

- The first term of a sequence is called T_1, the second term is T_2 and so on.
- To predict what will come next in a sequence, we must find a rule that links one number or diagram with the next.

In our course we study three main types of numeric sequences and their associated graphs.

1. **Linear sequences**, e.g. 2, 5, 8, 11, 14, ...

   A linear (arithmetic) sequence is formed by adding/subtracting the same amount to any term to get the next term. This 'same amount' is usually called the **common difference**, d.

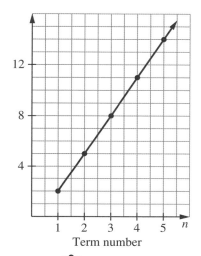

2. **Quadratic sequences**, e.g. 0, 5, 8, 9, 8, 5, 0

   Sequences that have an nth term containing n^2 as the highest power are called quadratic sequences. We use a technique called differencing, explained later in this chapter, when working with quadratic sequences.

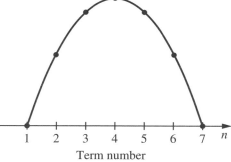

3. **Exponential sequences**, e.g. 2, 4, 8, 16, ...

   In these sequences, when we look for a term-to-term rule, we find that it involves multiplying (by 2 in this case).

   When terms are calculated by multiplying, the sequence is always exponential.

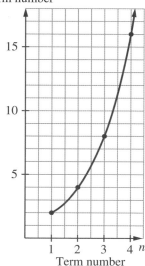

Predicting the pattern

Aspects of mathematics are about pattern. The following questions are simple and numeric.

Find the next three terms in each sequence.

(i) 2, 5, 8, _____, _____, _____

(ii) 16, 12, 8, _____, _____, _____

(iii) 1, 4, 9, 16, _____, _____, _____

key point

A sequence in which you go from term to term by adding (or subtracting) the same number each time is called an arithmetic sequence or linear sequence.

Solution

(i) 2, 5, 8, . . .

+3   +3

2   5   8   11   14   17

(ii) 16, 12, 8, . . .

−4   −4

16   12   8   4   0   −4

key point

Arithmetic sequence with common difference −4.

(iii) 1, 4, 9, 16, . . .

$(1)^2, (2)^2, (3)^2, (4)^2, (5)^2, (6)^2, (7)^2$

1,   4,   9,   16,   25,   36,   49

key point

A much tougher question: this is not an arithmetic sequence. Some outside-the-box thinking makes the solution simple. It is in fact a quadratic sequence.

exam focus

This question was very badly answered by candidates. It was awarded a total of 5 marks for all nine correct answers. However, it is important to note that 3 of those marks were awarded for **any one** of those nine correct answers.

x represents an even number.

Explain why $x + 2$ is the next even number.

Solution

The pattern for even numbers is identified on the following number line.

> **key point**
>
> The common difference between each even number is $+2$.

20   22   24   26   28

Hence, we observe that for any even number, x, the next even number is $x + 2$.

The first eight Fibonacci numbers are 0, 1, 1, 2, 3, 5, 8, 13.

Fibonacci numbers are found by adding the previous two numbers to get the next one.

5 was found by adding the two numbers before it $(2 + 3)$.

8 was found by adding the two numbers before it $(3 + 5)$.

13 was found by adding the two numbers before it $(5 + 8)$.

Find the next three Fibonacci numbers:

0, 1, 1, 2, 3, 5, 8, 13, _____, _____, _____.

Solution

$$0 \quad 1 \quad 1 \quad 2 \quad 3 \quad 5 \quad 8 \quad 13$$
$$T_1 \quad T_2 \quad T_3 \quad T_4 \quad T_5 \quad T_6 \quad T_7 \quad T_8 \quad T_9 \quad T_{10} \quad T_{11}$$

$T_9 = T_8 + T_7 = 13 + 8 = 21$

$T_{10} = T_9 + T_8 = 21 + 13 = 34$

$T_{11} = T_{10} + T_9 = 34 + 21 = 55$

> **exam focus**
>
> Some questions on pattern are neither linear, quadratic nor exponential.

In a number pyramid you add the two numbers in the lower blocks to find the number in the block above (for examples, 2 + 3 = 5).

Complete the number pyramid by filling in the empty spaces.

Solution

First

Then

Finally

This question was extremely badly answered by candidates. As a result it was awarded only 5 marks for all seven correct answers. However, it is important to note that 3 of those marks were awarded for **any one** of those seven correct answers.

Example

The pattern indicated below shows the first six rows of Pascal's triangle.

```
                1       1
            1       2       1
        1       3       3       1
    1       x       6       4       1
  y     5       10      10      5       1
a       b       c       d       e       f       g
```

Write down the value of the letters x, y, a, b, c, d, e, f and g.

Solution

> **The first and last number in every line = 1 and each number is the sum of the two numbers above it in the preceding row.**

$1 = a = y = g$

Then
```
            1       3       3       1
        1       x       6       4       1
            = 1 + 3
            = 4
```

Finally
```
1           5           10          10          5           1
  1       b           c           d           e           f           1
      = 1 + 5     = 5 + 10    = 10 + 10   = 10 + 5    = 5 + 1
      = 6        = 15        = 20        = 15        = 6
```

Kevin has saved €20. He gets €7 a week for doing jobs at home.
He spends €2 on sweets every week and saves the rest in a piggybank.

(i) How much money has he saved at the end of week 1?

(ii) Complete the table to show how his savings grow in the first five weeks.

	Week 1	Week 2	Week 3	Week 4	Week 5
€20		€30			

(iii) Write down a formula (in words) to represent the amount he has saved at the end of each week.

(iv) Kevin would like to buy a mobile phone costing €100. Use your formula to find out how many weeks he needs to save to have enough money to buy the phone.

(v) Kevin stops buying the sweets after five weeks. How much can he save each week after that?

(vi) Kevin thinks he can buy his phone three weeks sooner with the extra savings. Do you agree with Kevin? Explain your answer.

Solution

(i) 20 + 7 − 2 = 20 + 5 = €25 saved at end of week 1

(ii)
20	= 20
20 + 5	= 25
20 + 5 + 5	= 30
20 + 5 + 5 + 5	= 35
20 + 5 + 5 + 5 + 5	= 40
20 + 5 + 5 + 5 + 5 + 5	= 45

However, the examiner also accepted an answer of €5 saved in part **(i)**.

	Week 1	Week 2	Week 3	Week 4	Week 5
€20	€25	€30	€35	€40	€45

(iii) €20 plus €5 for each week

= €20 + €5 multiplied by the week number

= €20 + €5n, where n is the week number

= 20 + 5n

(iv) 20 + 5n = 100   (an equation in disguise)

      5n = 100 − 20   (subtract 20 from both sides)

      5n = 80

       n = 16   (divide both sides by 5)

After 16 weeks of saving, Kevin has enough money to buy the phone.

(v) Sweets cost Kevin €2 each week. If he stops buying sweets he has an extra €2 to save. €5 + €2 = €7.

(vi) In 13 weeks he saves

20 + (5 + 5 + 5 + 5 + 5) + (7 + 7 + 7 + 7 + 7 + 7 + 7 + 7)

= 20 + five (5) + eight (7)

= 20 + 25   + 56

= € 101   yes agree with Kevin.

The above work is my explanation.

 key point

3 weeks sooner is (16 − 3) = 13 weeks

 exam focus

This question was awarded a total of 24 marks.

As candidates found part **(iii)** and part **(vi)** very difficult, each part was awarded only 2 marks.

Candidates did better on parts **(i)**, **(ii)**, **(iv)** and **(v)**. These four parts were awarded 5 marks each.

It is vital that you attempt each part of every question in this exam.

Predicting pattern from given graphs and diagrams

Not all patterns are numeric. For example, a series of shapes are made using matches.

How many matches will be needed for the 6th shape?

Answer: 5, 9, 13, 17, 21 then 25 matches for the 6th shape, that is four extra matches each time.

Three experiments on temperature are done in the science lab.
Pupils record and plot the temperature of each experiment
each hour, for five hours.

Science Experiments

In experiment A, the temperature doubles every hour.

In experiment B, the temperature increases by 2° every hour.

In experiment C, the temperature increases by 3° each hour for three hours and
then remains constant.

Identify each experiment by its number.

Solution

In experiment B the temperature increases by +2° every hour. This is what we call
a linear (straight line) sequence. Hence, B is associated with graph 3.

Experiment C is also linear but stops increasing after three hours.

Hence, C is associated with graph 2.

By elimination, A is associated with graph 1.

key point

Graph 1 is exponential
(more on this later in
the chapter).

exam focus

5 marks were awarded for matching the letters A, B, C, with the correct
positions.

Remember to attempt everything.

Melissa bought a horse in 2007 for €500. She took the horse to the sales each year for three years to have it valued but did not sell. She recorded the values on the graph below.

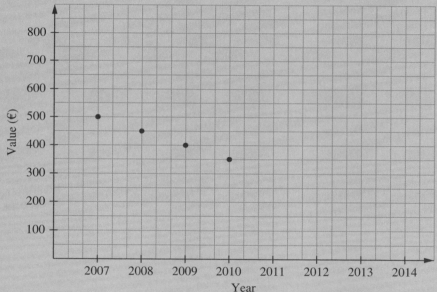

(i) Use a line to join the points on the graph.

(ii) If the pattern continued, what was the horse worth in 2011?

(iii) How much does the horse lose in value each year?

(iv) Melissa will sell the horse when it reaches a value of €200. If the pattern continues, in what year will she sell the horse?

(v) James bought a horse for €700 in 2007. His horse loses value at a constant rate. It was worth €100 in 2011. Mark these two points on the graph above, and join them with a straight line.

(vi) In what year will the two horses have the same value? What is that value?

(vii) Louise examines the graph and says "looking at the slopes of the lines, I can tell which horse loses value faster". Explain in your own words what Louise means.

This question links pattern and coordinate geometry (a topic usually examined in Paper 2).

Solution

(i)

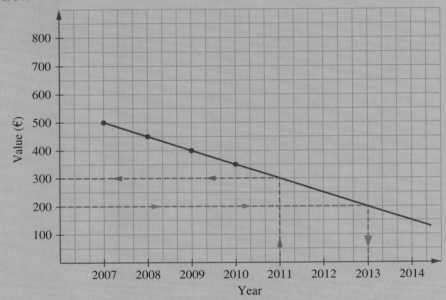

(ii) €300 (reading from the graph ---▶---)

(iii) 500, 450, 400, 350 . . . suggests minus €50 each year.

(iv) The horse is worth €200 in 2013 (reading from the graph ---▶---)

Full marks awarded for answers in the range €275 to €325.

(v)

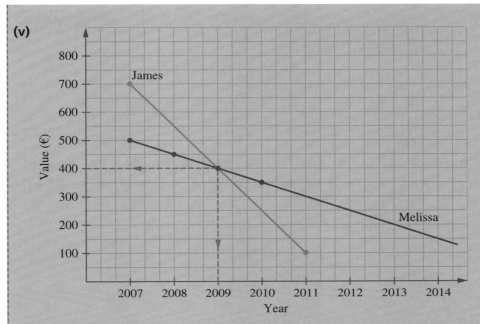

(vi) Reading from the graph above, the two horses have the same value in 2009 and that value was €400.

The point of intersection of the two lines gives the answers to part **(vi)**.

(vii) The (downward) slope of Melissa's line tells Louise that the value of Melissa's horse is decreasing. However, the much steeper (downward) slope of James's line tells Louise that the value of his horse is decreasing at a faster rate.

This question was awarded a total of 29 marks.

The very easy part **(i)** was awarded 2 marks.

The badly answered part (vii) was also awarded 2 marks.

Parts **(ii)**, **(iii)**, **(iv)**, **(v)** and **(vi)** were awarded 5 marks each.

Example

In the following pattern, the first figure represents 1 dot, the second represents 3 dots, etc.

This pattern can also be described in function notation:

$f(1) = 1,$ $f(2) = 3,$ $f(3) = 6$, etc.

(i) Hence or otherwise, write down:

     (a) $f(4)$ (b) $f(6)$ (c) $f(7)$ (d) $f(8)$

(ii) Write down the value of q where $f(q) = 55$.

Solution

(i) From the diagram we construct the following table.

Figure	1	2	3	4	5	6	7	8	9	10
Number of dots	1	3	6	10	15	21	28	36	45	55

Notice:

     (a) $f(4) = 10$ (b) $f(6) = 21$ (c) $f(7) = 28$ (d) $f(8) = 36$

(ii) By observation from the table constructed in part (i):

     $f(10) = 55,$ which means $q = 10$.

Exam questions will often link topics, as above where pattern is linked with function notation.

Differencing (change)

Many investigative and problem-solving questions lead to a sequence of numbers. The technique of differencing is useful in certain situations involving sequences. To observe an application of differencing, we apply the technique to the sequence 3, 7, 13, 21, 31, 43, ...

To find the first difference:

- Subtract the first number in the sequence from the second.
- Subtract the second number in the sequence from the third.
- Subtract the third number in the sequence from the fourth and so on.

The second differences can be found by taking the difference of the first differences. The third differences can then be found and so on again.

Hence we find:

	First difference (first change)	Second difference (change of change)	Third difference (change of change of change)
$T_1 = 3$			
	4		
$T_2 = 7$		2	
	6		0
$T_3 = 13$		2	
	8		0
$T_4 = 21$		2	
	10		0
$T_5 = 31$		2	
	12		
$T_6 = 43$			

key point

- When the first difference is the same value each time, the pattern is referred to as a linear pattern. When graphed, a linear pattern is a straight line.
- When the second difference is the same value each time, the pattern is referred to as a quadratic pattern. When graphed, a quadratic pattern will be a curve and not a straight line.

First difference

Second difference

If the second difference is not constant, the pattern is **not** quadratic.

Example

A stone is dropped from the top of a building and lands on the ground below. The total distance that it fell from the top of the building was recorded at 1-second intervals. It landed on the ground after 5 seconds.
The results are shown in the table.

Time (seconds)	Distance (metres)
0	0
1	6
2	24
3	54
4	96
5	150

 (i) What is the height of the building?

 (ii) Do these results form a linear relationship? Explain your answer.

(iii) Could these results be represented by a quadratic function? Explain your answer.

Solution

 (i) 150m (since the stone landed on the ground after 5 seconds and it had fallen 150m).

(ii) and (iii)

Not linear, as the first differences are not constant. However, since the second difference is constant, it is quadratic.

Example

The Fibonacci sequence of numbers is 1, 1, 2, 3, 5, 8, 13, 21, 34, . . .
Show that the sequence of first differences for the Fibonacci sequence is also the Fibonacci sequence.

Solution

Term	1	1	2	3	5	8	13	21	34
First difference (first change)		0	1	1	2	3	5	8	13

By observing the first difference calculation we see this new sequence is also Fibonacci.

key point

The second (and all subsequent) differences are also the Fibonacci sequence in the above example.

Exponential sequences

The syllabus restricts our study of exponential sequences to two types: doubling and trebling. Below is an example and a graph of each type.

Type 1   Doubling
    6, 12, 24, 48, 96, . . .

Type 2   Trebling
    2, 6, 18, 54, 162, . . .

Exponent is another word for power, e.g. 3^1, 3^2, 3^3, 3^4, . . . In everyday language exponential growth is used to indicate very rapid growth.

Remember: exponent = power = index

Example

A lily growing in a pond doubles in size every five days. After 20 days it has covered half the pond. How long does it take to cover the full pond?

Solution

A graph will help us see the pattern. The percentage covered doubles every five days.

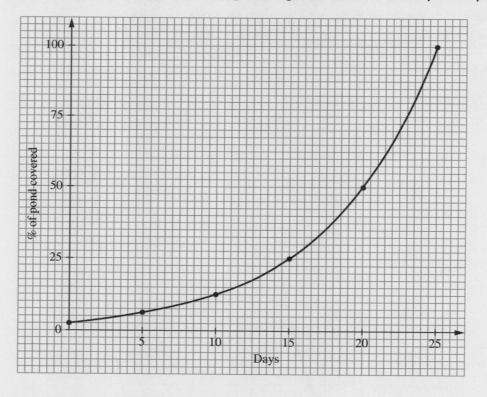

After 20 days 50% of pond is covered.
After 25 days 100% of pond is covered.

Given the right conditions of food, moisture and warmth, some bacteria can divide into two every hour. This is known as binary fission and is especially important in the food industry in order to avoid food poisoning. The diagram below shows the growth by division of one bacterium.

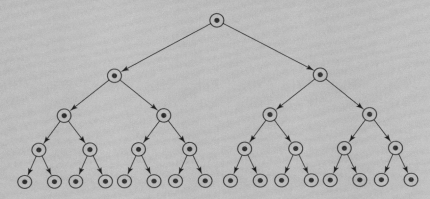

(i) How many bacteria will this single one have become after growing for five hours?

(ii) Complete this table.

Time in hours	0	1	2	3	4	5	6	7
Number of bacteria	2^0	2^1			2^4			

(iii) By noting $2^0 = 1$; $2^1 = 2$; $2^2 = 4$; $2^3 = 8$; etc.

Draw the graph in the domain $0 \leq t \leq 7$, where t is the time in hours.

(iv) Use your graph to estimate the number of bacteria present after $5\frac{1}{2}$ hours.

(v) Use the table of results from part **(ii)** to write down an expression for the number of bacteria present after one day.

Solution

(i) After five hours there are $2^5 = 2 \times 2 \times 2 \times 2 \times 2 = 32$ bacteria.

(ii)

Time in hours	0	1	2	3	4	5	6	7
Number of bacteria	2^0	2^1	2^2	2^3	2^4	2^5	2^6	2^7

(iii)

Time in hours	0	1	2	3	4	5	6	7
Number of bacteria	1	2	4	8	16	32	64	128

(iv) From the above graph we follow ↑ and estimate that there are 47 bacteria after $5\frac{1}{2}$ hours.

(v) After 24 hours there are 2^{24} bacteria = 16,777,216.

1 day = 24 hours

11 Sets

aims

☐ To be familiar with set symbols and set notation.

☐ To be able to construct and interpret Venn diagrams.

☐ To know the meaning of terms such as subsets, cardinal number, set difference and complement of a set.

☐ To be able to identify whether the commutative property holds in situations involving sets.

☐ To gain the necessary skills to solve problems concerning two sets.

☐ To be able to apply sets in the many different topics where it may be examined, e.g. probability, number theory.

Basic revision of sets terminology

1. A set is a well-defined collection of objects.

   The set of whole numbers between $2\frac{1}{4}$ and $5\frac{1}{3}$ is a well-defined set, but for the example the set of good actors is not. Different people will give different answers.

2. Equal sets

   Two sets are equal if they contain exactly the same elements.

   If $E = \{1, 3, 8, 9\}$ and $F = \{9, 3, 1, 8\}$, then $E = F$.

3. Element of a set.

   If $E = \{$The first five letters in the alphabet$\}$, then

   (i) d is an element of E and is written as $d \in E$

   (ii) y is not an element of E and is written as $y \notin E$

4. The universal set (U)

   The set from which all other sets being considered is called the universal set, U.

5. If every element of a set E is also an element of a set F, then E is said to be a subset of F. This is written as $E \subset F$.

6. Union of two sets $(E \cup F)$

   The union of two sets is found by putting together in a new set all the elements of E and F without repeating an element. It is written as $E \cup F$.

   If $E = \{b, p, q, y\}$ and $F = \{a, b, e, y\}$, then $E \cup F = \{a, b, e, p, q, y\}$.

When listing the elements of a set, place the elements between chain brackets { } and separate them with commas. An element is never repeated and the order of the elements is **not** important.

7. Intersection of two sets $(E \cap F)$

   The intersection of two sets E and F is the set of elements that are in **both** E and F.

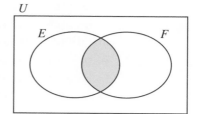

8. The complement of a set (E')

   The complement of a set E is the set of elements in the universal set U which are **not** in E.

   It is written as E'.

Some set notation is given in the booklet of formulae and tables, which is available to you in the examination.

exam Q

The Venn diagram represents the sets:

Natural numbers $\mathbb{N}$

Integers $\mathbb{Z}$

Rational numbers $\mathbb{Q}$

(i) Enter the following numbers in the correct sections of the Venn diagram.

   (a) 4   (d) $\dfrac{10}{3}$

   (b) −3   (e) −7·9

   (c) 0   (f) −25

(ii) Hence or otherwise, shade the empty set.

Solution

Using the number sets in the booklet of formulae and tables or from the chapter on number systems we write:

exam focus

This question links sets and number systems.

exam Q

$A = \{p, q, r\}$

Write down a subset of A that has: **(i)** one element **(ii)** two elements.

Solution

$A = \{p, q, r\}$

(i) Subsets of A that have one element are:

$\{p\}$ or $\{q\}$ or $\{r\}$ (any one will do).

(ii) Subsets of A that have two elements are:

$\{p, q\}$ or $\{p, r\}$ or $\{q, r\}$ (any one will do).

Set difference

To illustrate set difference, we consider two sets E and F where

$E = \{a, b, p, q, x, y\}$ and $F = \{a, b, c, d\}$.

If we remove from set E all the elements which are in set F, we have E less F.

E less F is denoted by $E \backslash F$.

We then write $E \backslash F = \{p, q, x, y\}$.

We may illustrate set difference by Venn diagrams as follows:

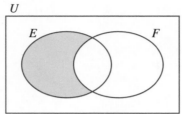

Shaded area is $E \setminus F$

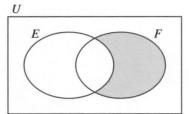

Shaded area is $F \setminus E$

Example

(i) From the Venn diagram list the elements of:

    (a) $R \cup S$ (b) $S \cup R$

    (c) $R \setminus S$ (d) $S \setminus R$

(ii) Using the results from **part (i)** explain why:

    (a) Union of sets is commutative

    (b) Set difference is not commutative

Solution

(i) (a) $R \cup S = \{e, \theta, \mu, \beta\}$

    (b) $S \cup R = \{\beta, \mu, e, \theta\}$

    (c) $R \setminus S = \{e, \theta\}$

    (d) $S \setminus R = \{\beta\}$

(ii) (a) $R \cup S = S \cup R$ Note: When the order is reversed the answers are the same, so union of sets is commutative.

    (b) $R \setminus S \neq S \setminus R$ Note: When the order is reversed the answers are not the same, so set difference is not commutative.

key point

It is vital to know the meaning of the word 'commutative'. Commutative means we get the same result when the order is reversed.

The cardinal number of a set (#)

The number of elements in a set is called the cardinal number of the set.

The symbol # is used to denote cardinal number.

If $E = \{p, q, r, s\}$,   then $\#E = 4$.

Example

From the given Venn diagram, answer the following:

(i) A (ii) A'

(iii) $\#A$ (iv) $\#A'$

Solution

(i) $A = \{4, 6, 2\}$ (ii) $A' = \{5, 3\}$

(iii) $\#A = 3$ (iv) $\#A' = 2$

Recall that A', the complement of A, is all elements **not** in A.

Example

In the given Venn diagram, each dot represents an element. Write down:

(i) $\#E$ (ii) $\#(E \cap F)$

(iii) $\#(F \backslash E)$ (iv) $\#F'$

(v) $\#[U \backslash (E \cup F)]$ (vi) $\#[(F \backslash E) \cup (E \backslash F)]$

Solution

(i) $\#E = 3$ (ii) $\#(E \cap F) = 2$

(iii) $\#F \backslash E = 5$ (iv) $\#F' = 4$

(v) $\#[U \backslash (E \cup F)] = \#[(E \cup F)'] = 3$

(vi)

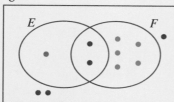

$\#[(F \backslash E) \cup (E \backslash F)] = 6$

Numerical problems on two sets

If some of the elements are not in any of the given sets, then we must introduce the universal set. Also, in many problems we may have to use a variable, say, x, to represent the number of elements in a region.

The sports played by a set of girls *G* and a set of boys *B* in a Limerick school are shown in the Venn diagram.

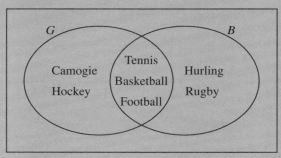

(i) Describe the region of the diagram where camogie and hockey are located.

(ii) Describe the region of the diagram where tennis, basketball and football are located.

(iii) (a) In the Venn diagram, shade the set $A \cup B$.

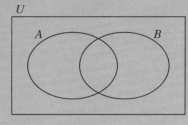

(b) In the Venn diagram, shade the set $(A \cup B)'$, where $(A \cup B)'$ is the complement of $A \cup B$.

This question was awarded a total of 25 marks, with 10 of those marks awarded for the very easy and well answered part **(ii)**. Remember to attempt every part of every question, and write **something** down . . . you never know how marks will be awarded!

Solution

(i) Girls only or $G \setminus B$ or $U \setminus B$.

(ii) $G \cap B$ or sports played by both girls and boys.

(iii) (a)

$(A \cup B)$

(b)

$(A \cup B)'$

key point

Unfortunately, candidates mixed up $A \cup B$ and $A \cap B$. Be sure you know the difference between A union B and A intersection B.

exam Q

The universal set $U = \{1, 2, 3, 4, 5, 7, 10, 11, 13, 17, 19, 20\}$.

A is the set of prime numbers between 1 and 20. B is the set of factors of 20.

(i) List the elements of the set A.

$A = \{$,   ,   ,   ,   ,   , $\}$

(ii) List the elements of the set B.

$B = \{$,   ,   ,   , $\}$

(iii) Fill in the Venn diagram below, placing all elements of U in the correct regions.

(iv) List the elements of $A \cap B$.

$A \cap B = \{$ $\}$

(v) Complete the sentence below.

If an element is in the region $A \cap B$, it has two properties: it is a prime number and it is _____.

(vi) The number 16 is added to the universal set. Place 16 in the correct region in the Venn diagram in part **(iii)** and explain why you placed it there.

Solution

(i) $A = \{2, 3, 5, 7, 11, 13, 17, 19\}$

(ii) $B = \{1, 2, 4, 5, 10, 20\}$

(iii)

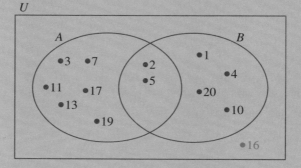

(iv) $A \cap B = \{2, 5\}$

(v) If an element is in the region $A \cap B$, it has two properties: it is a prime number and it is a factor of 20.

(vi) 16 (in red colour above in the Venn diagram) is not a prime number and is not a factor of 20. It is outside $A \cup B$ but is in U.

Many candidates mixed up union (∪) and intersection (∩).

This question was awarded a total of 24 marks, with generous marks (partial credit) for any correct work. Parts **(i)** + **(v)** were each awarded 2 marks and parts **(ii)**, **(iii)**, **(iv)** and **(vi)** each awarded 5 marks.

U = {Natural numbers from 1 to 10 inclusive} K = {Factors of 6}
L = {Even numbers}

(i) Fill in the Venn diagram below:

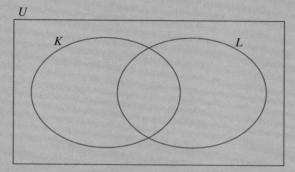

(ii) Use ✓ to indicate whether each of the following statements is true or false.
Give a reason for each answer.

(a) $K \cap L = \{\quad\}$

True ☐   False ☐

This question was awarded
a total of 20 marks: 5 marks
for each part.

(b) $K \neq L$

True ☐   False ☐

(c) $K \cup L = U$

True ☐   False ☐

Solution

(i)

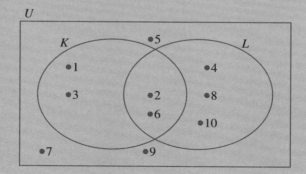

(ii) (a) False, because $K \cap L = \{2, 6\}$

(b) True, because $\{1, 2, 3, 6\} \neq \{2, 4, 6, 8, 10\}$.

(c) False, because
$\{1, 3, 2, 4, 6, 8, 10\} \neq \{1, 2, 3, 4, 5, 6, 7, 8, 9, 10\}$
or $K \cup L$ does not include 5, 7 or 9, which are in U.

exam focus

Many good candidates lost up to 6 marks here because they did **not** include a reason with their (correct) answers.

exam Q

A leisure centre has 110 members. The weights room (W) is used by 82 members and the swimming pool (S) is used by 57 members. 15 members do not use either facility.

Draw a Venn diagram and complete it to show the number of members in each part of each set.

key point

Solution

Let the number of members who use both $= x$,

i.e. $\#(W \cap S) = x$.

The number using the weights room only $= 82 - x$

The number using the swimming pool only $= 57 - x$

The total number of members

$= \#(U)$

$= 110$

When working with Venn diagrams, always work from the centre outwards.

U

W $\quad\quad\quad$ S

$[82 - x]$ $\quad [x] \quad$ $[57 - x]$

$[15]$

Hence, $\quad [82 - x] + [x] + [57 - x] + [15] = 110$

$82 - x + x + 57 - x + 15 = 110$

$154 - x = 110$

$154 - 110 = x$

$44 = x$

Finally:

In a survey of tourists, 1,611 said they had visited the Cliffs of Moher and 946 had visited the Giant's Causeway. 113 had visited neither.

What is   **(i)** The greatest number that could have been surveyed

(ii) The smallest number that could have been surveyed?

Solution

(i) Let x represent the number of tourists who visited both.

The total number surveyed is $\#U = (946 - x) + x + (1{,}611 - x) + 113$
$$= 2{,}670 - x$$

The smallest value that x can have is zero.

Hence, the greatest number surveyed = $\#U = 2{,}670 - 0 = 2{,}670$.

(ii) The biggest value x can have is 946.

Hence, the least number surveyed = $\#U = 2{,}670 - 946 = 1{,}724$.

In a survey of 30 students in a class it was found that:

21 own a mobile phone (*M*) and 11 own a computer (C).
6 own both a mobile phone and a computer.

(i) Represent this information in the Venn diagram below.

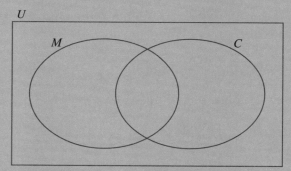

(ii) A student is selected at random from the class. What is the probability that the student owns:

(a) A computer

(b) A mobile phone but not a computer

(c) Neither a mobile phone nor a computer?

Solution

(i)

$21 - 6 = 15$ Mobile phone only

$11 - 6 = 5$ Computer only

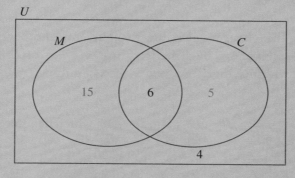

Finally, $15 + 6 + 5 = 26$. With 30 students in the class, we state 4 have neither.

(ii)

(a) P (Student has a computer) $= \dfrac{11}{30}$

(b) P (Student has a mobile phone but not a computer) $= \dfrac{15}{30} = \dfrac{1}{2}$

(c) P (Student has neither) $= \dfrac{4}{30} = \dfrac{2}{15}$.

exam focus

This question links sets and probability. A more detailed study of these types of questions on probability may be found in the chapter on probability in *Less Stress More Success Paper 2*.

12 Functions

aims
- ☐ To learn what a function is and how to recognise one.
- ☐ To become familiar with the notation associated with functions.
- ☐ To be able to solve problems involving functions.

A function is a rule that changes one number (input) into another number (output). Functions are often represented by the letters f, g, h or k. We can think of a function, f, as a number machine which changes an input, x, into an output, $f(x)$.

Input

Output

$f(x)$, which denotes the output, is read as 'f of x'.

key point

A function is also called a **mapping** or simply a **map**.

For example, let's represent the function 'double input and then add 5' by the letter f. This can be written as:

$$f{:}x \rightarrow 2x + 5 \quad \text{or} \quad f(x) = 2x + 5 \quad \text{or} \quad y = 2x + 5$$
$$(\text{input, output}) = (x, f(x)) = (x, 2x + 5) = (x, y)$$

One number is mapped onto another number. In the above example, x is mapped onto $2x + 5$, usually written as $f: x \rightarrow 2x + 5$.

A function connects every input (x) in the domain to an output $(f(x))$ in the range.

A function is another way of writing an algebraic formula that links input (x) to output $(f(x))$.

key point

Note the different notations for function:

$f: x \rightarrow$

$f(x)$

y

Types of functions	
Linear	$f: x \rightarrow ax$ or $f: x \rightarrow ax + b$
Quadratic	$f: x \rightarrow ax^2 + bx + c$
Exponential	$f: x \rightarrow ab^x$

Input number

If $f: x \rightarrow 2x + 5$, then $f(3)$ means 'input 3 into the function', i.e. it is the result of applying the function f to the number 3.

$$f(3) = 2(3) + 5 = 6 + 5 = 11 \qquad (\text{input} = 3, \text{output} = 11)$$
$$(\text{input}, \text{output}) = (3, f(3)) = (3, 11)$$

key point

A function performs the exact same procedure to each input number and produces only one output number for each input number.

The set of input numbers is called the **domain**. The set of output numbers is called the **range**.

The set of **all possible outputs** is called the **codomain**.

In general, the range is a subset of the codomain. However, sometimes the range and the codomain are the same.

Consider the function f shown:

$f = \{(1, a), (2, b), (3, d), (4, d)\}$

from set X to set Y.

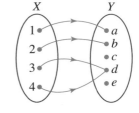

Domain: The set of elements from which the arrows leave: $\{1, 2, 3, 4\}$.
Range: The set of elements where the arrows arrive: $\{a, b, d\}$.
Codomain: The **possible** set of elements into which the arrows go: $\{a, b, c, d, e\}$.

Example

$P = \{(1, 5), (2, 8), (2, 9), (3, 10)\}$

Write out the domain and range of P.

Solution

The domain is the inputs: Domain = $\{1, 2, 2, 3\}$
Domain = $\{1, 2, 3\}$ (do not enter 2 twice)

The range is the outputs: Range = $\{5, 8, 9, 10\}$

$T = \{(1, p), (2, p), (3, q), (4, r)\}$

Write out the domain and range of T.

Solution

The domain is the inputs: Domain = {1, 2, 3, 4}

The range is the outputs: Range = {p, p, q, r}

                              Range = {p, q, r}   (do not enter p twice)

To recognise if a mapping represents a function:

- If any element in the domain has no arrow, then it is **not** a function.
- If any element in the domain has more than one arrow leaving it, it is **not** a function.
- Therefore, a mapping represents a function if there is **exactly one arrow leaving every element in the domain**.

Example

State whether each of the following mapping diagrams is a function.
Give a reason for your answer in each case.

(i)   (ii)

(iii)   (iv)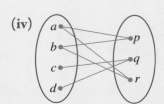

Solution

 (i) Is a function, as each element of the domain (inputs) has only one output.

(ii) Is not a function, as input x has two outputs. Also, input z has no output.

(iii) Is not a function, as one element in the domain, input b, has no output.

(iv) Is not a function, as inputs a and b have more than one output.

Example

Find the value of $f(-3)$ when $f(x) = 2 - 5x$.

Solution

$$f(x) = 2 - 5x$$
$$f(-3) = 2 - 5(-3)$$
$$f(-3) = 2 + 15$$
$$f(-3) = 17$$

key point

Substituting and solving equations are vital skills for you to have when working with functions. Working with functions follows the same procedure as substituting and solving equations in Algebra. These were covered in earlier chapters.

Example

A function is given by $f(x) = 2x - 1$. Find the value of $f(2) + f(-1)$.

Solution

$$f(x) = 2x - 1$$
$$f(2) = 2(2) - 1 \qquad\qquad f(-1) = 2(-1)-1$$
$$f(2) = 4 - 1 \qquad\qquad\quad f(-1) = -2 - 1$$
$$f(2) = 3 \qquad\qquad\qquad f(-1) = -3$$

Therefore, $f(2) + f(-1) = 3 + (-3)$
$$f(2) + f(-1) = 3 - 3$$
$$f(2) + f(-1) = 0$$

exam Q

$f(x) = 3x - 5$. Find the value of:

(i) $f(7)$ (ii) $f(-2)$

Solution

(i) $f(x) = 3x - 5$

   $f(7) = 3(7) - 5$

   $f(7) = 21 - 5$

   $f(7) = 16$

(ii) $f(x) = 3x - 5$

   $f(-2) = 3(-2) - 5$

   $f(-2) = -6 - 5$

   $f(-2) = -11$

$f(x) = x^2 + x - 3$. Find the value of.

(i) $f(3)$ **(ii)** $f(-1)$

Solution

(i) $f(x) = x^2 + x - 3$

   $f(3) = (3)^2 + (3) - 3$

   $f(3) = 9 + 3 - 3$

   $f(3) = 9$

(ii) $f(x) = x^2 + x - 3$

   $f(-1) = (-1)^2 + (-1) - 3$

   $f(-1) = 1 - 1 - 3$

   $f(-1) = -3$

Example

A function is given by $f(x) = 4x - 3$. If $f(x) = 21$, find x.

Solution

$$f(x) = 4x - 3$$
$$21 = 4x - 3 \qquad \text{(let } f(x) = 21)$$
$$21 + 3 = 4x - 3 + 3 \qquad \text{(add 3 to both sides)}$$
$$24 = 4x \qquad \text{(simplify)}$$
$$\frac{24}{4} = x \qquad \text{(divide both sides by 4)}$$
$$6 = x$$

Example

A function f is defined as $f(x) = 3x - 2$.

Find the missing numbers, p, q and r.

Solution

$$f(x) = 3x - 2$$

$$f(4) = 3(4) - 2$$

$$p = 12 - 2$$

$$\therefore \quad p = 10$$

$$f(x) = 3x - 2$$

$$f(-2) = 3(-2) - 2$$

$$q = -6 - 2$$

$$\therefore \quad q = -8$$

To find r, we are given an equation in disguise

Output $= 4$, find input r:

$$f(x) = 3x - 2$$

$$f(r) = 3r - 2$$

$$4 = 3r - 2$$

$$4 + 2 = 3r - 2 + 2$$

$$6 = 3r$$

$$2 = r$$

Example

A function f is defined as $f: x \longrightarrow 2x - 5$. Complete the following four couples:

(i) (3,)   (ii) (−3,)   (iii) (,3)   (iv) (,7)

Solution

(i) $f: x \longrightarrow 2x - 5$ (3,)   Input $= 3$ Output $= ?$

When $x = 3$, find y: $f(3) = 2(3) - 5$

$$f(3) = 6 - 5$$

$$f(3) = 1$$

Therefore, the couple is (3, 1).

(ii) $f: x \longrightarrow 2x - 5$ (−3,)   Input $= -3$ Output $= ?$

When $x = -3$, find y: $f(-3) = 2(-3) - 5$

$$f(-3) = -6 - 5$$

$$f(-3) = -11$$

Therefore, the couple is (−3, −11).

(iii) $f: x \longrightarrow 2x - 5$ (,3)   Input $= ?$ Output $= 3$

When $y = 3$, find x: $3 = 2x - 5$

$$3 + 5 = 2x$$

$$8 = 2x$$

$$4 = x$$

Therefore, the couple is (4, 3).

(iv) $f{:}x \rightarrow 2x - 5$ (, 7)   Input = ?   Output = 7

When $y = 7$, find x: $7 = 2x - 5$

$$7 + 5 = 2x$$
$$12 = 2x$$
$$6 = x$$

Therefore, the couple is $(6, 7)$.

A school is planning a trip to a local museum. They are taking the school's mini-bus. It will cost €42 for parking for the bus during the day. Tickets to enter the museum are €16·50 per student.

(i) Find the total cost of the trip in terms of n, where n equals the number of students who go on the trip.

(ii) Find the total cost of the trip for 20 students.

(iii) Find the cost of the trip, per student, if 14 students go on the trip.

(iv) If the total cost of the trip came to €339, how many students went on the trip?

key point

Solution

(i) n = Number of students

Cost = Cost of parking + Ticket per student

$C = €42 + €16·50(n)$

Notice that this is actually a fairly straightforward pattern question.

(ii) Find the cost when $n = 20$: $C = €42 + €16·50(n)$

$$C = €42 + €16·50(20)$$
$$C = €42 + €330$$
$$C = €372$$

Therefore, the trip will cost €372 for a group of 20 students.

(iii) Find the cost when $n = 14$: $C = €42 + €16·50(n)$

$$C = €42 + €16·50(14)$$
$$C = €42 + €231$$
$$C = €273$$

Therefore, the trip will cost €273 for a group of 14 students.

Cost per person = €273 ÷ 14 = €19·50 per person

(iv) Find n when $C = 339$: $C = €42 + €16·50(n)$

$$€339 = €42 + €16·50(n)$$
$$339 - 42 = 16·50(n)$$
$$297 = 16·50(n)   (÷ 16·50)$$
$$18 = n$$

Therefore, 18 students went on the trip.

A ball is thrown into the air from the roof of a building. Its height above the ground, h (measured in metres), at any given time after the ball is thrown, t (measured in seconds), can be modelled using the quadratic function $h = -4t^2 + 20t + 23$.

(i) Find the height of the ball above the ground after 3 seconds.

(ii) Find the height of the ball above the ground after 4·5 seconds.

(iii) Find the two times when the height of the ball is 39m.

(iv) Find the height of the building.

Solution

(i) Find h when $t = 3$:
$$h = -4t^2 + 20t + 23$$
$$h = -4(3)^2 + 20(3) + 23$$
$$h = -4(9) + 60 + 23$$
$$h = -36 + 83$$
$$h = 47$$

Therefore, after 3 seconds, the ball was at a height of 47m.

(ii) Find h when $t = 4·5$:
$$h = -4t^2 + 20t + 23$$
$$h = -4(4·5)^2 + 20(4·5) + 23$$
$$h = -4(20·25) + 90 + 23$$
$$h = -81 + 113$$
$$h = 32$$

Therefore, after 4·5 seconds, the ball was at a height of 32m.

(iii) Find t when $h = 39$m:
$$h = -4t^2 + 20t + 23$$
$$39 = -4t^2 + 20t + 23$$
$$4t^2 - 20t - 23 + 39 = 0$$
$$4t^2 - 20t + 16 = 0 \qquad \text{(divide both sides by 4)}$$
$$t^2 - 5t + 4 = 0$$
$$(t - 4)(t - 1) = 0$$
$$t - 4 = 0 \quad \text{or} \quad t - 1 = 0$$
$$t = 4 \, \text{sec} \qquad\qquad t = 1 \, \text{sec}$$

(iv) The ball is released when time is 0 seconds.

Find h when $t = 0$:
$$h = -4t^2 + 20t + 23$$
$$h = -4(0)^2 + 20(0) + 23$$
$$h = -4(0) + 0 + 23$$
$$h = 0 + 23$$
$$h = 23$$

The ball is at height 23m when it is released, therefore the height of the building was 23m.

aims

☐ To be able to graph functions of various forms.
☐ To be able to use the graphs to find the solution to given questions.

Graphing functions

To graph a function, find points which satisfy the function by substituting values in for x and finding the corresponding y-values. Plot these points and join them up to obtain the graph of the function.

key point

To better understand the graphs of functions, you should practise graphing functions on a graphing calculator or graphing software, such as Geogebra (free to download from www.geogebra.org).

Linear functions

A linear function is usually given by $f: x \rightarrow ax + b$, where $a, b \in \mathbb{Q}, x \in \mathbb{R}$.
To graph a linear function you need two points.

If the coefficient of the x part is positive ($a > 0$), the graph is **increasing**:	If the coefficient of the x part is zero ($a = 0$), the graph is **horizontal**:	If the coefficient of the x part is negative ($a < 0$), the graph is **decreasing**:
e.g. $y = 2x + 3$	e.g. $y = 3$	e.g. $y = -2x + 3$

key point

Graphing linear functions is covered extensively under the topic of Coordinate Geometry of the Line, which can be found in *Less Stress More Success for Junior Certificate Project Maths Paper 2*. There is also a connection between linear functions and arithmetic patterns.

{(2, 4), (3, 6), (4, 8), (5, 10)} are four couples of a function *f*.

(i) Plot the four couples.

(ii) The function *f* is derived by a rule. Suggest a rule for *f*.

(iii) On your diagram in **(i)**, plot and label two other couples which could be gotten from the same rule.

Solution

(i) Plotting the points given (plotted in blue on the graph):

The points form a straight line, so the line joining them would be a linear function.

Plotting points: (*x*, *y*)
= (horizontal, vertical)
= (over/back, up/down)
= (input, output)

(ii) In the first couple, *x* = 2 and *y* = 4.
In the second couple, *x* = 3 and *y* = 6.
In the third couple, *x* = 4 and *y* = 8.

Looking at the pattern we can see that the *y*-values are twice the *x*-values in each case. So the rule is $y = 2x$.

(iii) More couples which follow the rule $y = 2x$ are. (1, 2) or (6, 12).

These points are marked in red on the diagram in **(i)**.

Part **(i)** was worth 15 marks, with 10 marks awarded for correctly plotting any **one** point.

Part **(ii)** was worth 5 marks, with 3 marks awarded for any correct step.

Part **(iii)** was worth 5 marks, with 3 marks awarded for plotting either of the two points.

Example

(i) Graph the function $y = 2x + 1$ in the domain $-2 \le x \le 3$.

(ii) Using your graph, find the value for y when $x = 2$.

Solution

(i) In order to graph a linear function, find the two points at the end of each line segment.

$$y = 2x + 1$$

If input, $x = -2$

Output, $y = 2(-2) + 1$

$y = -4 + 1$

$y = -3$

$(-2, -3)$

If input, $x = 3$

Output, $y = 2(3) + 1$

$y = 6 + 1$

$y = 7$

$(3, 7)$

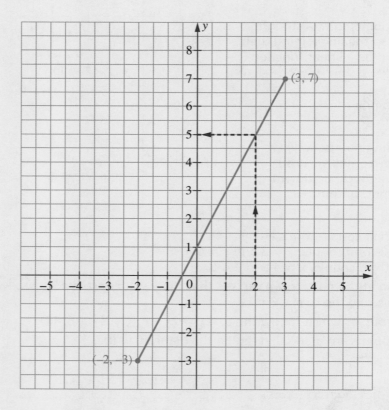

(ii) From the graph, when $x = 2$, $y = 5$ (the blue line on the graph).

Example

(i) On the same axes and scales, graph the functions $f : x \longrightarrow 3x + 3$ and $g : x \longrightarrow -x + 3$ in the domain $-2 \leq x \leq 2$.

(ii) From your graph, estimate the point where $f(x) = g(x)$ (the point where the two lines intersect).

Solution

(i) On the same axes and scales, graph the functions $f : x \longrightarrow 3x + 3$ and $g : x \longrightarrow -x + 3$ in the domain $-2 \leq x \leq 2$.

$$f(x) = 3x + 3$$

$x = -2$:	$x = 2$:
$f(x) = 3(-2) + 3$	$f(x) = 3(2) + 3$
$y = -6 + 3$	$y = 6 + 3$
$y = -3$	$y = 9$
$(-2, -3)$	$(2, 9)$

$$g(x) = -x + 3$$

$x = -2$:	$x = 2$:
$g(x) = -(-2) + 3$	$g(x) = -(2) + 3$
$y = 2 + 3$	$y = -2 + 3$
$y = 5$	$y = 1$
$(-2, 5)$	$(2, 1)$

Graphing the lines:

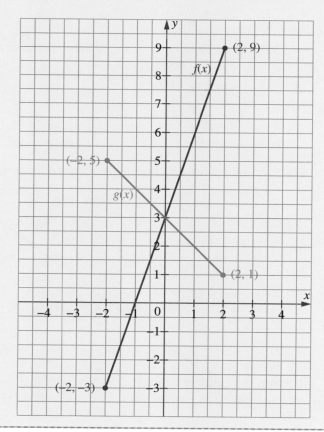

(ii) The lines intersect (cross) at the point $(0, 3)$.

Therefore, $f(x) = g(x)$ at the point $(0, 3)$.

A taxi has a base starting charge of €4. The passenger is then charged an additional €1·50 for every kilometre travelled.

(i) Write a function for the cost of a trip in terms of k where k is the number of kilometres travelled.

(ii) Graph the function in the domain from 0km to 16km.

(iii) Use your graph to find the cost of a trip which lasted 12km.

(iv) Use your graph to find the distance covered during a trip which cost €13.

Solution

(i) Cost of a trip = Base charge of €4 + €1·50 per kilometre
$$c = €4 + €1·50(k)$$
$$c = 4 + 1·5(k)$$

(ii) Find the start and end points.

When $k = 0$km:
$$c = 4 + 1·5(k)$$
$$c = 4 + 1·5(0)$$
$$c = 4 + 0$$
$$c = 4$$
Start point: (0, 4)

When $k = 16$km:
$$c = 4 + 1·5(k)$$
$$c = 4 + 1·5(16)$$
$$c = 4 + 24$$
$$c = 28$$
End point: (0, 28)

Graph these points and join them to graph the function:

It is very important to label the axes. This makes the graph meaningful.

A linear function can be represented by:

y = starting value + (rate of growth)x

This is the same as a linear or arithmetic pattern.

It is also the same as the equation of a line.

y = mx + c

Where *m* = rate of growth = slope

   c = starting value = *y*-intercept

(see booklet of formulae and tables)

(iii) From the graph (red line), when number of kilometres *k* = 12, the cost equals €22.

(iv) From the graph (green line), when the cost equals €13, the number of kilometres equals 6.

Quadratic functions

A quadratic function can be given in the form $f: x \rightarrow ax^2 + bx + c$, where $a \in \mathbb{N}, b, c \in \mathbb{Z}$, $x \in \mathbb{R}$ and $a \neq 0$.

Because of its shape, quite a few points are needed to accurately graph a quadratic function.

key point

The values where the graph of a quadratic function crosses the *x*-axis are known as the roots of the function. These are the values you get when you solve the quadratic equation formed, by letting the function equal zero.

Example

Draw a graph of the function $f : x \rightarrow x^2 + 3x - 1$ in the domain $-5 \le x \le 2$.

Solution

Complete a table.

x	$x^2 + 3x - 1$	y
−5	$(-5)^2 + 3(-5) - 1$	9
−4	$(-4)^2 + 3(-4) - 1$	3
−3	$(-3)^2 + 3(-3) - 1$	−1
−2	$(-2)^2 + 3(-2) - 1$	−3
−1	$(-1)^2 + 3(-1) - 1$	−3
0	$(0)^2 + 3(0) - 1$	−1
1	$(1)^2 + 3(1) - 1$	3
2	$(2)^2 + 3(2) - 1$	9

The ordered pairs are $(-5, 9), (-4, 3), (-3, -1), (-2, -3),$ $(-1, -3), (0, -1), (1, 3)$ and $(2, 9)$.

Plot these points and join them up to graph the function $f(x)$.

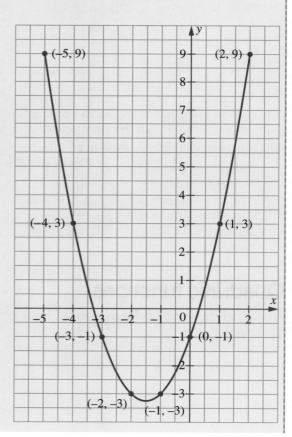

Alternative method to finding the points:

$$f(-5) = (-5)^2 + 3(-5) - 1 = 9 \qquad f(-1) = (-1)^2 + 3(-1) - 1 = -3$$
$$f(-4) = (-4)^2 + 3(-4) - 1 = 3 \qquad f(0) = (0)^2 + 3(0) - 1 = -1$$
$$f(-3) = (-3)^2 + 3(-3) - 1 = -1 \qquad f(1) = (1)^2 + 3(1) - 1 = 3$$
$$f(-2) = (-2)^2 + 3(-2) - 1 = -3 \qquad f(2) = (2)^2 + 3(2) - 1 = 9$$

The ordered pairs are $(-5, 9), (-4, 3), (-3, -1), (-2, -3), (-1, -3), (0, -1),$ $(1, 3)$ and $(2, 9)$.

exam focus

It is important that you show your workings when finding the outputs for the function. The 'Table' mode on the Casio calculator can be used to **check** these outputs. You can input the function and the domain of inputs and then the calculator will give all outputs. It's a good idea to practise this function on your calculator to become familiar with it.

exam Q

(i) Complete the following table for the function
$f: x \rightarrow x^2 - 3x - 2$ in the domain $-2 \le x \le 4, x \in \mathbb{R}$.

(ii) Using the values obtained in **(i)**, draw the graph of
the function $f: x \rightarrow x^2 - 3x - 2$ in the domain
$-2 \le x \le 4, x \in \mathbb{R}$.

Solution

(i) $f(x) = x^2 - 3x - 2$

$f(-2) = (-2)^2 - 3(-2) - 2 = 4 + 6 - 2 = 8$
$f(-1) = (-1)^2 - 3(-1) - 2 = 1 + 3 - 2 = 2$
$f(0) = (0)^2 - 3(0) - 2 = 0 + 0 - 2 = -2$
$f(1) = (1)^2 - 3(1) - 2 = 1 - 3 - 2 = -4$
$f(2) = (2)^2 - 3(2) - 2 = 4 - 6 - 2 = -4$
$f(3) = (3)^2 - 3(3) - 2 = 9 - 9 - 2 = -2$
$f(4) = (4)^2 - 3(4) - 2 = 16 - 12 - 2 = 2$

x	f(x)	(x, f(x))
−2	8	(−2, 8)
−1		
0		
1		
2		
3		
4		

(ii) Graph of the function:

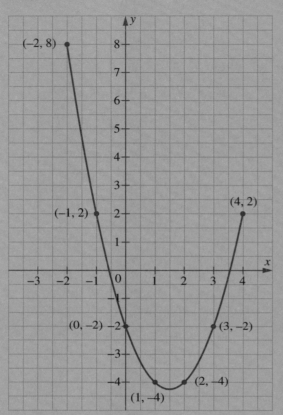

x	f(x)	(x, f(x))
−2	8	(−2, 8)
−1	2	(−1, 2)
0	−2	(0, −2)
1	−4	(1, −4)
2	−4	(2, −4)
3	−2	(3, −2)
4	2	(4, 2)

Part **(i)** was worth 15 marks, with 7 marks awarded for correctly evaluating any one correct value for $f(x)$ and 12 marks for evaluating four values of $f(x)$ correctly.

Part **(ii)** was worth 15 marks, with 7 marks awarded for correctly plotting any one point and 12 marks for correctly plotting any four points.

Make sure you attempt all parts. There are no marks for blanks!

Example

The graph shows the functions
$f(x) = x^2 - 9$ and $g(x) = x - 3$.
Use the graph to find the points
where $f(x) = g(x)$.

Solution

From the graph, we can see that the
functions cross, or intersect, at the
points $(-2, -5)$ and $(3, 0)$.

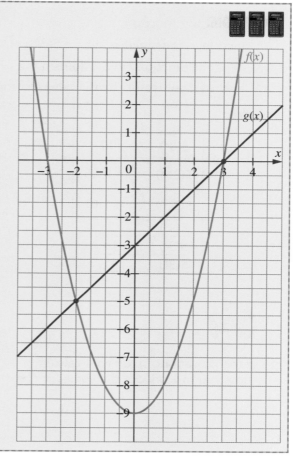

Exponential functions

On our course, an exponential function will be given in the form $f: x \rightarrow a2^x$ or
$f: x \rightarrow a3^x$, where $a \in \mathbb{N}$ and $x \in \mathbb{R}$.

**For exponential graphs in the
form $f(x) = a2^x$ or $f(x) = a3^x$:**

The graph is increasing and the
curve intersects the y-axis at the
point $(0, a)$. This point is called
the focal point.

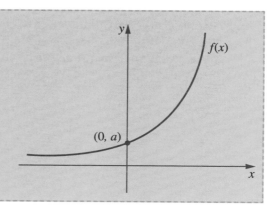

Example

The function, f, is defined as $f: x \rightarrow 5(3^x)$.

(i) Graph the function f in the domain $-2 \leq x \leq 2$.

(ii) Use the graph to estimate the value of x for which $f(x) = 30$.

Solution

(i)

x	$5(3^x)$	$f(x)$
-2	$5(3^{-2})$	$\dfrac{5}{9} = 0 \cdot 56$
-1	$5(3^{-1})$	$\dfrac{5}{3} = 1 \cdot 67$
0	$5(3^0)$	5
1	$5(3^1)$	15
2	$5(3^2)$	45

key point

Use the power button on your calculator to help you to work out the values of $f(x)$.

(ii) Go to 30 on the y-axis, go horizontally across to the graph and then drop a vertical line down to find the corresponding value of x.

When $f(x) = 30$, $x = 1 \cdot 6$.

The number of bacteria, $B(t)$, in a sample after t hours can be represented by the model:

$$B(t) = 50(2^t).$$

(i) Graph the number of bacteria for the first 5 hours.

(ii) Use the graph to estimate the number of bacteria present after 4·5 hours.

(iii) Use to graph to estimate after how many hours there are 600 bacteria present in the sample.

Solution

(i)

t	$50(2^t)$	$B(t)$
0	$50(2^0)$	50
1	$50(2^1)$	100
2	$50(2^2)$	200
3	$50(2^3)$	400
4	$50(2^4)$	800
5	$50(2^5)$	1,600

(ii) From the graph:
when $t = 4·5$ hours,
$B(4·5) = 1,120$
(red line).

(iii) From the graph:
when $B = 600$, $T = 3·6$ hours
(green line).

14 Rounding, Estimates, Ratio, Direct Proportion and Graphs

☐ To be able to present numerical answers to the degree of accuracy specified.

☐ To be able to make approximations and estimates of calculations.

☐ To learn how to use ratio and proportion.

☐ To draw and interpret graphs using direct proportion.

Rounding

In the exam we are sometimes asked to round our answers.

The number 9·4837 = 9, correct to the nearest whole number

= 9·5, correct to one decimal place

= 9·48, correct to two decimal places

= 9·484, correct to three decimal places

The number 68,176 = 70,000, correct to one significant figure

= 68,000, correct to two significant figures

= 68,200, correct to three significant figures

key point

When expressing a whole number correct to a given number of significant figures, zeros at the end of the number are not counted, but must be included in the final result. All other zeros are significant, e.g. 90,426 = 90,400 correct to three significant figures.

exam Q

(i) Write the following numbers correct to the nearest ten.

121   195   504

(ii) Write the following numbers correct to three decimal places.

105·5555   2·173   0·0264

(iii) Write the following numbers correct to two significant figures.

2,920   159   0·0336

Solution

(i) $121 \rightarrow 120$

$195 \rightarrow 200$

$504 \rightarrow 500$

(ii) $105{\cdot}5555 \rightarrow 105{\cdot}556$

$2{\cdot}173 \rightarrow 2{\cdot}173$

$0{\cdot}0264 \rightarrow 0{\cdot}026$

(iii) $2{,}920 \rightarrow 2{,}900$

$159 \rightarrow 160$

$0{\cdot}0336 \rightarrow 0{\cdot}034$

exam focus

Candidates had no idea how to answer this question. As a result, a **total** of 5 marks was awarded for all nine correct answers, with 3 marks awarded for any one correct answer! Remember, always write down **something**. This type of question may be asked again.

Changing units in the metric system

We are often required to change from one unit to another, as illustrated in the following exam question.

exam focus

The booklet of formulae and tables may help.

exam Q

(i) Change 5,000g to kilograms.

(ii) Change 2·7m to centimetres.

(iii) Change 8,000cm³ to litres.

(iv) Change 4m² to cm².

Solution

(i) $5{,}000g = \dfrac{5{,}000}{1{,}000} = 5kg$

(ii) $2{\cdot}7\,m = 2{\cdot}7 \times 100 = 270cm$

(iii) $8{,}000cm^3 = \dfrac{8{,}000}{1{,}000} = 8\ell$

(iv) $1m = 100cm \Rightarrow 1m^2 = 100 \times 100cm^2$

$4m^2 = 4 \times 100 \times 100cm^2 = 40{,}000cm^2$

key point

The booklet of formulae and tables gives us

Kilo = 10^3 ($=1{,}000$) and

Centi = $10^{-2}\left(=\dfrac{1}{100}\right)$, that is,

$1m = 100cm$

key point

$1\ell = 1{,}000cm^3$

You must know this.

exam focus

Each part above was worth 5 marks, with 3 marks awarded in each part for any one correct piece of work. Keep writing.

Rounding and changing units in the metric systems are skills required for both papers in the exam. For more, see the section on the area and volumes chapter in the *Less Stress More Success Paper 2* book.

Estimates

There are many occasions when it is either desirable or necessary to round off large or small numbers to a reasonable degree of accuracy. With the widespread use of calculators, it is important that we have some estimate of the answer we expect to get. Then we will know whether the answer shown on the calculator is reasonable or not.

Jack had to estimate the cost of 396 teddy bears. The calculation he used was 396 × 27·25.

Without a calculator, Jack has to estimate the answer.

396 is approximately 400.
27·25 is approximately 27.

Hence, an approximate answer is 400 × 27 = €10,800.

Croke Park in Dublin holds 82,300 people when full.

During a football match a reporter estimated that the stadium was 40% full.

How many people were estimated to be at the game?

Give your answer correct to the nearest 100 people.

Solution

100% = 82,300

$1\% = \dfrac{82{,}300}{100} = 823$

40% = 823 × 40 = 32,920

To the nearest 100 people = 32,900.

Alternatively,

40% of the stadium = 82,300 × 0·40 = 32,920

Then to the nearest 100 people we write 32,900.

$40\% = \dfrac{40}{100} = \dfrac{4}{10} = 0\cdot4$

(i) Karen went to a shop to buy five magazines. She had €10 to spend. She made an estimate of the total cost by correcting the price of each magazine to the next highest euro. The magazines cost €1·95, €1·99, €3·59, €1·40 and 99 cent. Work out her estimate.

(ii) Based on the estimate, would she think she had enough money?

(iii) Work out the exact cost of the magazines.

(iv) Suggest what you think is a better method for estimating the total cost of the magazines. Give a reason for your answer.

Solution

(i) €1·95 → 2·00

€1·99 → 2·00

€3·59 → 4·00

€1·40 → 2·00

€0·99 → 1·00

Total = €11·00

(ii) Since her estimate is €11 and she has €10 to spend, she concludes that she does not have enough money.

If Karen's answer to part **(i)** was €10 or less, she would in part **(ii)** conclude that she had enough money.

This type of question, which has two opposite and contradictory answers where both are awarded full marks, often appears on the exam. **Always** write down your opinion and back it up with your work clearly shown. This will maximise your final result.

(iii) 1·95 + 1·99 + 3·59 + 1·40 + 0·99 = €9·92

(iv) It would be more accurate if Karen rounded to the nearest whole number.

This is likely to give a better estimate, as some prices will round up and some will round down.

The above question was worth a total of 25 marks.

It was not well answered.

However, part **(iii)** was easy and well answered. It was awarded 10 marks. Even if you cannot do the first part of a question, you should continue on and attempt all parts.

Eight people ate at a restaurant. Each meal was approximately the same cost. The bill was €128. A service charge of 10% was then added.

Michelle said, '€15 each is enough to pay the bill and service charge'.

(i) Do you agree with her estimate?   Yes ☐ No ☐
Give a reason for your answer.

(ii) Can you suggest a better estimate? Give a reason for your answer.

This question was awarded a total of 15 marks. The easy part **(i)** was awarded 10 of those marks. Be sure to answer each part of each question to the best of your ability and you will do very well.

Solution

(i) €15 each from 8 people = €120.

This is not enough to pay the bill of €128.

We do not agree with Michelle's estimate. No ☑

10% of €128 = €12·80

(ii) The total bill = 128 + 12·80 = €140·80

Shared equally by 8 people means €140·80 ÷ 8 = €17·60.

Hence, any amount greater than or equal to €17·60 is a better estimate. The calculations above are my reason.

Ratio and proportion

Ratios are used to compare quantities. We can be asked to divide quantities in a given ratio and solve problems on proportion.

€400 is shared between Mary and Tom in the ratio 7:3. How much does each receive?

Solution

7 + 3 = 10 parts

So: 1 part = $\dfrac{€400}{10}$ = €40

7 parts = 40 × 7 = €280 for Mary

3 parts = 40 × 3 = €120 for Tom

A sum of money was divided in the ratio 3:2. The larger amount was €39. What was the total amount of money?

Solution

This question gives us an equation in disguise.

3 parts = €39

$$1 \text{ part} = \frac{39}{3} = €13$$

Then 3 parts + 2 parts = 5 parts = Total amount

Hence, 5 parts = 13 × 5 = €65 is the total amount of money.

Example

€5,580 is shared between Fred and Ciara in the ratio of their ages. Fred is three times as old as Ciara.

(i) Write down the ratio of their ages.

(ii) How much money does each receive?

(iii) How much money would Fred have to give to Ciara so that they would have equal amounts?

Solution

(i) Fred:Ciara = 3:1

(ii) 3 + 1 = 4 is the total number of parts.

$$1 \text{ part} = \frac{5,580}{4} = €1,395, \quad \text{hence 3 parts} = 1,395 \times 3 = €4,185$$

Ciara gets €1,395 and Fred gets €4,185.

(iii)

key point

For both to have equal parts, the calculation is $\frac{5,580}{2} = €2,790.$

Hence, for Fred and Ciara to have equal amounts, Fred must give Ciara 4,185 − 2,790 = €1,395.

Directly proportional graphs

If a graph of two variables is a straight line through the origin, then one variable is **directly proportional** to the other. This means that if one variable changes, then the other also changes by the same ratio.

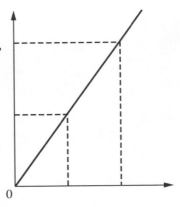

0

Example

Noah is filling this cylinder with water.
The water is being delivered from the tap at the rate of 120ml/sec.
Noah times how long it takes to fill the cylinder.

Height of water (cm)	6	12	18	24	30	36
Time taken (sec)	1.2	2.4	3.6	4.8	6.0	7.2

(i) Draw a graph of height against time.

(ii) Use your graph to find the height of the water after 5 seconds.

(iii) How long does it take for the water to reach a height of 20cm?

Solution

(i)

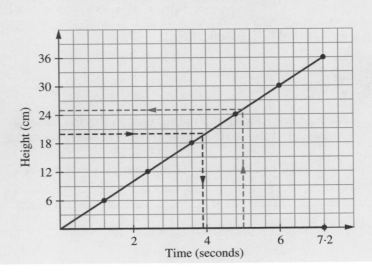

(ii) From the graph after 5 seconds the height is 25cm.

(iii) From the graph a height of 20cm is reached after 3·9 seconds.

key point

The rate of flow of 120ml/sec is not required in our solution.

Example

The previous question based on Noah filling the cylinder with water may be presented in the following way:

Height (*h*)

36cm

7·2 secs

Time (*t*)

Use the gradient of the graph to find the rule connecting the two variables.

Solution

The gradient = The slope = m = $\dfrac{\text{Rise}}{\text{Run}} = \dfrac{36}{7·2} = \dfrac{360}{72} = 5$

key point

A gradient (slope) of 5 means that in this example, the level of the water increases by 5cm every second.

In which of these graphs is *q* directly proportional to *t*?

(i)

(ii)

(iii)

(iv)

Solution

(i) Is not a straight line, hence not directly proportional.

(ii) Does not pass through the origin, hence not directly proportional.

(iii) A straight line through the origin indicates *t* and *q* are directly proportional.

(iv) Is not a complete straight line, hence not directly proportional.

15 Distance, Speed, Time and Graphs of Motion

☐ To learn how to solve problems involving distance, speed and time.
☐ To be able to apply your knowledge and skills to solve problems on graphs of motion.
☐ To be able to tell the story of a graph of motion.

Metric system

It is important to be able to convert units in the metric system.

A swimming pool is 50m in length. Mary swims 25 lengths of the pool. What distance does Mary swim

(i) in metres **(ii)** in kilometres?

Solution

(i) 50m × 25 lengths = 1,250m

(ii) 1,250m = $\dfrac{1,250}{1,000}$ km = 1·25km

1,000 m = 1 km

Converting minutes to hours

To convert minutes to hours, **divide by** 60.

For example, 36 minutes $= \dfrac{36}{60} = \dfrac{6}{10} = \dfrac{3}{5} = 0·6$ hours.

The following occur often and are easy to memorise

15 minutes $= \dfrac{1}{4}$ hour; 20 minutes $= \dfrac{1}{3}$ hour; 10 minutes $= \dfrac{1}{6}$ hour.

Converting hours to minutes

To convert fractions, or decimals, of an hour to minutes, **multiply by** 60.

For example; $\dfrac{2}{3}$ hour $= \dfrac{2}{3} \times 60 = \dfrac{120}{3} = 40$ minutes.

0·75 hour = 0·75 × 60 = 45 minutes

Distance, speed and time

There are three formulas to remember when dealing with problems involving distance (D), speed (S) and time (T). **Note:** Speed here means average speed.

1. Speed = $\dfrac{\text{Distance}}{\text{Time}}$ **2.** Time = $\dfrac{\text{Distance}}{\text{Speed}}$ **3.** Distance = Speed × Time

key point

It can be difficult to remember these formulae. To help you remember, consider the triangle on the right. By covering the quantity required (*D, S* or *T*), any of the three formulas above can be found by inspection.

Distance

Speed × Time

Common units of speed

1. Kilometres per hour, written as km/h.
2. Metres per second, written as m/s.

exam focus

Marks may be lost if you do not include units in your answers, where appropriate.

exam Q

Cormac went by car from Limerick to Cork, a journey of 100km. He travelled at an average speed of 80km/h.

(i) How many hours and minutes did it take Cormac to complete the journey?

(ii) Cormac left Limerick at 11:15. At what time did he arrive in Cork?

(iii) Cormac's car used 1 litre of petrol for every 16km travelled. On that day, petrol cost 155 cent per litre. Find the cost of the petrol used on Cormac's journey from Limerick to Cork. Give your answer to the nearest euro.

Solution

(i) Time = $\dfrac{\text{Distance}}{\text{Speed}} = \dfrac{100}{80} = 1{\cdot}25$ hours

$\qquad = 1{\cdot}25$ hours $= 1\frac{1}{4}$ hours $= 1$ hour and 15 minutes

(ii)

11:15	Left Limerick
+ 1:15	
12:30	Arrives in Cork

(iii) Number of litres required $= \dfrac{\text{Distance travelled}}{16}$

$\qquad\qquad\qquad\qquad\qquad = \dfrac{100}{16}$

$\qquad\qquad\qquad\qquad\qquad = 6{\cdot}25$ litres

Cost $= 6{\cdot}25 \times 155$ cents $= 968{\cdot}75$ cents $= €9{\cdot}6875$

Answer: petrol costs €10 to the nearest euro.

Peter travelled 50km to a football match and he returned home by the same route when the match was over.

(i) Peter travelled to the match at an average speed of 60km/h. How many minutes did the journey to the match take?

(ii) Peter arrived at the match at 17:35. At what time did he leave from home to travel to the match?

(iii) Peter took 75 minutes to travel home from the match. Calculate the average speed, in km/h, for this journey.

Solution

(i) Time = $\dfrac{\text{Distance}}{\text{Speed}} = \dfrac{50}{60} = \dfrac{5}{6}$ hours

$\qquad$ Time $= \dfrac{5}{6} \times 60$ minutes

$\qquad$ Time $= 50$ minutes

(ii) Arrived at 17:35

$\qquad$ Travel time 50 minutes

key point

Transfer one hour into the minutes column.

17:35		16:95	
− 50	$\Rightarrow$	− 50	
		16:45	This is the time Peter left home

(iii) 75 minutes to travel 50km

1 minute to travel $\dfrac{50}{75}$ km

60 minutes to travel $\dfrac{50 \times 60}{75}$ km

The average speed for this journey is 40km/hour.

$\dfrac{50 \times 60}{75} = 40$ by calculator.

Example

This is a distance-time graph. Which of these descriptions best fits the graph?

(i) Bert walks to Ernie's house, stays a while and then returns home.

or

(ii) Bert walks up a hill, along a flat path, and then walks down a second hill.

Solution

(i) The answer is **(i)** because: we can say Bert travels from Ernie's house at a faster speed than he went to Ernie's house because the line on the graph is steeper in the third section.

The steepness of the lines on the above graph indicate speed. The steeper the line, the greater the speed. Also the line is flat for a while, indicating the distance did not change.

Olive cycled to the shop to get some milk for her tea. She cycled along a particular route and returned by the same route.
The graph below shows the different stages of her journey.

(i) How long did Olive stay in the shop?

(ii) How far from her home is the shop?

(iii) Compare the speed of her trip to the shop with her speed on the way home.

(iv) Write a paragraph to describe her journey.

Solution (i) and (ii)

Reading from the graph, Olive stayed in the shop for $35 - 20 = 15$ minutes.

Reading from the graph, Olive's home is 5km, or 5,000m, from the shop.

(iii) Speed to the shop

$$= \frac{\text{Distance}}{\text{Time}}$$

$$= \frac{5,000}{20}$$

$$= 250\text{m per minute}$$

Speed to her home

$$= \frac{\text{Distance}}{\text{Time}}$$

$$= \frac{5,000}{10}$$

$$= 500\text{m per minute}$$

Comparing the two speeds we conclude Olive travelled home at twice the speed.

(iv) Olive cycled for 20 minutes at a speed of 250m per minute on her way to the shop. She spent 15 minutes at the shop. On her return journey she cycled twice as fast and got home in 10 minutes.

The graph below shows some details about a journey Alex made by bicycle.

Alex waited for his friend before he set off on his journey.

(i) How long did he wait before setting out?

(ii) What was Alex's highest speed during the journey?

(iii) For what length of time was Alex travelling at the highest speed?

(iv) How far did Alex travel at the highest speed?

Solution

(i) Alex waited 5 minutes before setting out.

(ii) Alex had a highest speed of 20km per hour.

(iii)

Alex's Journey

Alex travelled at maximum speed from 25 minutes to 35 minutes, that is, for 10 minutes he travelled at maximum speed.

Candidates with answers close to the above answers were awarded full marks, e.g. for part **(iii)** 8 minutes was accepted, 11 minutes was accepted.

(iv) He travels at a speed of 20km per hour for 10 minutes.

Distance = Speed × Time

$$= 20 \times \frac{10}{60}$$

$$= \frac{200}{60}$$

$$= \frac{10}{3} \text{ km}$$

We write the time in hours.

This question was awarded a total of 25 marks, as follows:

(i) 10 marks

(ii) 5 marks

(iii) 5 marks

(iv) 5 marks

It is worth noting that the highest mark was given for the easiest question. Remember to write down **something** in each of the spaces provided for answers on the exam paper.

Example

Match each explanation to the correct graph.

(i) Rebecca walks part of the way to the shop and runs the rest of the way. She completes her shopping and runs all the way back home.

(ii) Bren walks to the shop and does some shopping. On the way home, being tired, Bren stops for a rest. He then walks very slowly the rest of the way home.

(iii) Noah goes for a walk to the post-box, posts his letter and returns home. He walks at a constant speed in both directions.

(iv) Elaine walked to Carol's house and stayed for tea. After tea Carol gave her a lift home in her car.

P

Q

R

S

Solution

Rebecca walks part of the way to the shop and runs the rest of the way. She completes her shopping and runs all the way back home.

Explanation (i) matches graph P.

Notice that the flat section represents the time Rebecca spends in the shop.

Bren walks to the shop and does some shopping. On the way home, being tired, Bren stops for a rest. He then walks very slowly the rest of the way home.
Explanation (ii) matches graph S.

Notice that the two flat sections represent when Bren visits the shop and when he stops for a rest.

Noah goes for a walk to the post-box, posts his letter and returns home. He walks at a constant speed in both directions.
Explanation (iii) matches graph Q.
Notice that as Noah does not stop on his journey, there are no flat sections.

Elaine walks to Carol's house and stays for tea. After tea Carol gives her a lift home in her car.
Explanation (iv) matches graph R.
Notice that the line representing Elaine's journey home by car is much **steeper** than the line representing her walk to Carol's house. This is because she travels much **faster** by car.

16 Arithmetic and Financial Maths

☐ To handle calculations involving money.
☐ To learn how to calculate household bills and VAT.
☐ To learn how to convert currencies or foreign exchange.
☐ To learn how to calculate percentage profit or loss.
☐ To learn how to calculate compound interest.
☐ To learn how to calculate income tax and take-home pay.

Calculations with money

exam
Q

Kathy and Jack Byrne have four children. A family ticket for the cinema costs €19·50. A family ticket is for two adults and two children. A single adult ticket costs €7·25 and a single child ticket costs €4·50.

(i) What is the total cost of a family ticket and two child tickets?

(ii) If an individual ticket was bought for each member of the family, what would be the extra cost?

Solution

(i) A family ticket costs €19·50.

Two child tickets cost €4·50 × 2 = €9·00.

Total cost of a family ticket and two child tickets

= 19·50 + 9·00

= €28·50

(ii) Two adult tickets cost €7·25 × 2 = €14·50.

Four child tickets cost €4·50 × 4 = €18·00.

Total cost = €32·50.

The extra cost is given by

€32·50 − €28·50 = €4·00.

exam
focus

This question was awarded a total of 15 marks: 10 marks for part **(i)** and 5 marks for part **(ii)**. Take good care doing the calculations and full marks can be gained quickly and efficiently.

Pat is a waiter at a restaurant. He is paid €8·65 per hour. He can also get tips. Last week he worked for 22 hours. Pat's wages plus tips were €235·50 in total for the week.

How much did Pat make on tips last week?

Solution
Wages found by €8·64 × 22 hours = €190·08.
The tips are found by €235·50 − €190·08 = €45·42 in tips.

This question was awarded a total of 15 marks, with a minimum award of 7 marks for any one correct step. However, full marks must be your goal here.

Example
The price of a holiday is increased by 8% to €1,782. What was the original cost of the holiday?

Solution

100% = | Original cost of holiday | →(+8%) €1,782 | = 108%

We write
$$108\% = €1{,}782$$
$$1\% = \frac{1{,}782}{108}$$
$$100\% = \frac{1{,}782}{108} \times 100 = €1{,}650$$

Therefore, the original cost of the holiday was €1,650.

Household bills and VAT
Value-added tax, or VAT, is a government tax which is added to many of the things that we buy. VAT is usually expressed as a percentage. When dealing with problems involving percentages, it is very important to be able to convert a percentage to a decimal. A calculator is particularly useful in these situations.

key point

To find 25%, multiply by $0\cdot25 = \dfrac{25}{100} = \dfrac{1}{4}$

To find 110%, multiply by $1\cdot10 = \dfrac{110}{100} = \dfrac{11}{10}$

To find 13·5%, multiply by $0\cdot135 = \dfrac{135}{1,000} = \dfrac{27}{200}$

exam Q

Jack takes his car to a garage for a service and receives an itemised bill. Find the total cost of servicing the car.

Itemised bill for service	Cost
5 litres of oil at €4·20 per litre	
2 windscreen wiper blades at €4·50 per blade	
2 brake shoes at €28 each	
2 hours of labour at €60 per hour	
Subtotal (before VAT added)	
VAT @ 13·5%	
Total bill	

Solution

€4·20 × 5 = €21·00 for oil

€4·50 × 2 = €9·00 for wiper blades

€28 × 2 = €56·00 for brake shoes

€60 × 2 = €120   for labour

€206·00 subtotal

To calculate the VAT:

$$100\% = €206$$

$$1\% = \dfrac{206}{100} \qquad \text{(divide both sides by 100)}$$

$$\text{VAT} = 13\cdot5\% = \dfrac{206}{100} \times 13\cdot5 \qquad \text{(multiply both sides by 13.5)}$$

$$\text{VAT} = 13\cdot5\% = €27\cdot81$$

Total bill = 206·00 + 27·81 = €233·81

Example

A telephone bill, including VAT at 23%, came to €116·85. Calculate the
bill without VAT.

Solution

$$100\% = \boxed{\begin{array}{c}\text{Bill before VAT} \\ \text{is added on}\end{array}} \xrightarrow{+23\%} \boxed{€116\cdot85} = 123\%$$

We then write

$$123\% = €116\cdot85$$

$$1\% = \frac{116\cdot85}{123} \qquad \text{(divide both sides by 123)}$$

$$100\% = \frac{116\cdot85 \times 100}{123} \qquad \text{(multiply both sides by 100)}$$

The bill without VAT = 100% = €95·00.

Alex's gas bill gave the following data:

Unit type	Present reading	Previous reading	Unit price
Day rate	42,384	40,932	€0·1702
Night rate	16,528	15,791	€0·0951

(i) Calculate the total cost of the units used, to the nearest cent.

(ii) Alex also pays a standing charge of €28·12 and a levy of €6·38. VAT is charged
on all amounts. If the total amount of Alex's gas bill is €429·10, find the
amount of VAT.

Solution

(i) Number of units used = Present reading – Previous reading

Day rate	Night rate
Present reading: 42,384	Present reading: 16,528
Previous reading: 40,932	Previous reading: 15,791
1,452 units	737 units
× €0·1702	× €0·0951
Cost: €247·1304	Cost: €70·0887

Total cost of units: €247·1304 + €70·0887 = €317·2191 = €317·22

(ii) Charges:

Units: €317·22

Standing charge: €28·12

Levy: €6·38

Total of charges: €351·72

Total of bill = Total of charges + VAT

€429·10 = €351·72 + VAT

€77·38 = VAT

Currency exchange

If we travel to a country not in the eurozone, we generally change our euro, €, to the currency of that country.

If you see €1 = 125 yen, ¥, displayed in a bank, how do you convert ¥10,000 to €?

We write ¥125 = €1

$$¥1 = €\frac{1}{125}$$

$$¥10,000 = €\frac{1}{125} \times 10,000 = €80$$

key point

Put the currency required on the right-hand side of the equation.

Example

On a certain day, €1 = $1·42.

(i) How many dollars would you get for €750?

(ii) How many euros would you get for $9,585?

Solution

(i)   €1 = $1·42   (dollars on the right, because we want our answer in dollars)

€750 = $1·42 × 750   (multiply both sides by 750)

€750 = $1,065

(ii) $1·42 = €1   (euros on the right, because we want our answer in euros)

$$\$1 = €\frac{1}{1·42}$$ (divide both sides by 1·42)

$$\$9,585 = €\frac{1}{1·42} \times 9,585$$ (multiply both sides by 9,585)

$9,585 = €6,750

A hotel website gives the cost of staying for three nights in a hotel in Copenhagen as 2,925 Danish kroner.

(i) Find the cost in euro, given that €1 = 7·5 Danish kroner.

(ii) This cost includes a 5% service charge for the website company. Find, in euro, how much the hotel will get for the three-night stay. Give your answer to two decimal places.

Solution

(i) 7·5 Danish kroner = €1

1 Danish kroner = €$\dfrac{1}{7·5}$

2,925 Danish kroner = €$\dfrac{1}{7·5}$ × 2,925 = €390

(ii) The cost of €390 includes a 5% service charge.

105% = €390

1% = €3·714285

100% = €371·4285

Therefore, the hotel will receive €371·43.

Percentage profit and loss and selling price

Profit and loss are often given as a percentage of the cost price. This is useful when we need to compare profit or loss on different items. Percentage profit or loss is calculated with the following formulae:

$$\text{Percentage profit} = \frac{\text{Profit}}{\text{Cost price}} \times 100\%$$

$$\text{Percentage loss} = \frac{\text{Loss}}{\text{Cost price}} \times 100\%$$

Example

Compact discs are bought for €10 each and sold for €15·50 each. Find the profit made on 20 compact discs.

Solution

Profit per disc = €15·50 − €10 = €5·50.

Profit made on 20 discs = €5·50 × 20 = €110.

key point

Profit = Sell price − Buy price

Example

Rebecca bought a car for €15,880 and sold it for €19,850.
Calculate her profit as a percentage of

(i) the cost price

(ii) the selling price

Solution

Profit = 19,850 − 15,880 = €3,970

(i) Profit as a percentage of cost price

$$= \frac{\text{Profit}}{\text{Cost price}} \times 100$$

$$= \frac{3,970}{15,880} \times 100$$

$$= 25\%$$

(ii) Profit as a percentage of selling price

$$= \frac{\text{Profit}}{\text{Selling price}} \times 100$$

$$= \frac{3,970}{19,850} \times 100$$

$$= 20\%$$

An exam question may ask you to explain or comment on why profit as a percentage of cost price and selling price are not equal. The answer is because one is over cost price while the other is over selling price. The above example shows why this is so.

Discounts

A discount is a reduction in the selling price. A discount is typically given to encourage customers to buy a product or to pay for a product in advance or in cash.

$$\text{Percentage discount} = \frac{\text{Discount}}{\text{Selling price}} \times 100\%$$

Example

A shop sold a TV for €1,071. This included a 16% discount. Calculate the price of the TV before the discount was allowed.

Solution

$$100\% = \boxed{\begin{array}{c}\text{Original}\\\text{cost of TV}\end{array}} \xrightarrow{-16\%} \boxed{\text{€1,071}} = 84\%$$

We write $\quad 84\% = €1,071$

$$1\% = \frac{1,071}{84}$$

$$100\% = \frac{1,071}{84} \times 100 = €1,275$$

key point

$$100\% - 16\% = 84\%$$

Hence, the original cost of the TV was €1,275.

Example

The price of a laptop is €700. In a sale the price of this laptop is reduced to €595. What is the percentage reduction on the original price of the laptop?

Solution

key point

The selling price is the original price and **not** the sale price. Watch out for this.

$$\text{Discount} = 700 - 595 = €105$$

$$\text{Percentage discount} = \frac{\text{Discount}}{\text{Selling price}} \times 100\%$$

$$= \frac{105}{700} \times 100\% = 15\%$$

Interest

Interest is the sum of money that you pay for borrowing money or that is paid to you for lending money.

Example

€6,400 was invested for one year and amounted to
€6,624 at the end of that year. Calculate the rate of
interest per annum.

Solution

$$\text{Interest} = €6,624 - €6,400 = €224$$

$$\text{Rate of interest} = \frac{\text{Interest}}{\text{Sum invested}} \times 100\% = \frac{224 \times 100\%}{6,400} = 3\cdot 5\%$$

key point

Per annum = per year

A sum of money invested at 10% per annum interest amounts to €907·50
after one year. How much was invested?

Solution

$$100\% = \boxed{\begin{array}{c}\text{Amount} \\ \text{invested}\end{array}} \xrightarrow{+10\%} \boxed{€907\cdot 50} = 110\%$$

We then write $110\% = €907\cdot 50$

$$1\% = \frac{907\cdot 50}{110} \qquad \text{(divide both sides by 110)}$$

$$100\% = \frac{907\cdot 50}{110} \times 100 \qquad \text{(multiply both sides by 100)}$$

The amount invested $= 100\% = €825.$

Compound interest

The formula for calculating compound interest is
given in the booklet of formulae and tables.

$F = P(1 + i)^t$, where F = final value (amount)

P = principal

i = interest rate

t = number of years

key point

i is always given in decimal
form.

$i = 5\% = 0\cdot 05$

$i = 16\% = 0\cdot 16$

$i = 3\cdot 5\% = 0\cdot 035$, etc.

Final amount is
principal + interest.

With compound interest, the interest earned each year is added to the principal to form a new principal. This new principal earns interest in the next year and so on.

The examination questions will not require you to calculate compound interest beyond **three** years. The formula is very efficient when combined with a calculator. However, the formula does **not** work if:

(i) The interest rate, i, is changed during the time period or

(ii) Money is added or subtracted during the time period.

Example

Calculate the compound interest on €8,800 for three years at 5% per annum.

In this question we use the formula because the interest rate does not change, nor is any money added or subtracted.

Solution

Given $P = 8,800$, $i = 5\% = 0.05$ and $t = 3$

$$F = P(1 + i)^t$$
$$F = 8,800(1 + 0.05)^3$$
$$F = 10,187.1 \qquad \text{(using a calculator)}$$

Compound interest $= F - P = 10,187.1 - 8,800 = €1,387.10$

Walter borrows €5,000 for two years at 7% per annum compound interest. He repays €2,000 at the end of the first year.

How much must he repay at the end of the second year to clear his loan?

Solution

Principal for first year = 100% = €5,000

$$1\% = \frac{5,000}{100}$$

$$7\% = \frac{5,000}{100} \times 7 = €350$$

We cannot use the formula in this case.

At the end of the first year, Walter owes 5,000 + 350 = €5,350.

He then repays €2,000, which means the principal for the second year is €5,350 − €2,000 = €3,350.

Principal for the second year = 100% = €3,350

$$1\% = \frac{3,350}{100}$$

$$7\% = \frac{3,350}{100} \times 7 = €234\cdot5$$

At the end of the second year Walter owes €3,350 + €234·5 = €3,584·50.

To clear his loan he must repay €3,584·50.

Dermot has €5,000 and would like to invest it for one year.
A special savings account is offering an annual interest rate of 4%.

  (i) Find the interest he would earn in the year.

 (ii) Tax of 33% will be deducted from the interest earned. Find the tax (33%) on the **interest** from part **(i)**.

(iii) Find the amount of the investment at the start of the second year.

Solution

(i)   100% = 5,000

$$1\% = \frac{5,000}{100}$$

$$\text{Interest rate} = 4\% = \frac{5,000 \times 4}{100}$$

The interest is €200.

(ii) Interest paid = 100% = €200

$$1\% = \frac{200}{100}$$

Tax deducted = 33% = $\frac{200 \times 33}{100}$ = €66

(iii) Amount of investment at start of second year

= 5,000 + Interest − Tax

= 5,000 + 200 − 66

= €5,134

Example

Eoin invests €1,000 in the Bank of Rupt.

This bank pays an annual interest rate such that an investment doubles in value every two years.

Eoin thinks that the interest rate must be 50%, but his dad, Michael, disagrees. Who is correct? Justify your answer.

Solution

We calculate what €1,000 amounts to in two years at 50% compound interest per annum using the formula:

$F = P(1 + i)^t$

where P = €1,000

i = 50% = 0·50

t = 2

Then $F = 1,000 (1 + 0·50)^2$

$F = 1,000 (1·5)^2 = €2,250$

Since €2,250 is greater than €2,000 (which is double €1,000), we conclude that the interest rate is not 50%. (In fact, the interest rate paid by the bank is less than 50%.)

Michael is correct.

exam focus

The question does not ask for the interest rate, but to justify who, Eoin or Michael, is correct.

Income tax

The following two equations are very important when calculating income tax.

> Gross tax − Tax credits = Tax payable
>
> Net income = Gross income − Tax paid

Net income is also called take-home pay.

Carla's gross pay is €24,000. Her tax credit is €2,500. She pays income tax at the rate of 22%. What is her take-home pay?

Gross Pay	€24,000
Tax @ 22%	
Tax Credit	€2,500
Tax Due	
Take-home Pay	

Solution

$$100\% = 24,000$$

$$1\% = \frac{24,000}{100}$$

$$\text{Tax @22\%} = \frac{24,000 \times 22}{100} = 5,280 \qquad \text{(by calculator)}$$

$$\text{Tax due} = \text{Tax payable} - \text{Tax credit}$$

$$= 5,280 - 2,500$$

$$= 2,780$$

$$\text{Take-home pay} = \text{Gross pay} - \text{Tax due}$$

$$= 24,000 - 2,780$$

$$= €21,220$$

Answer

Gross Pay	€24,000
Tax @ 22%	5,280
Tax Credit	€2,500
Tax Due	2,780
Take-home Pay	21,220

(i) Cathy works in a bakery and earns €8·65 per hour. She works 40 hours a week. Find Cathy's gross pay for the week.

(ii) Cathy has to pay income tax at a rate of 20%. Find Cathy's gross tax.

(iii) She has a tax credit of €20 per week. Find Cathy's net tax.

(iv) How much per week is she left with?

(v) Cathy had €1,650 saved in the credit union at the beginning of a year. The credit union paid 4·5% interest on her money. Find the interest earned in that year.

(vi) Cathy wants to use this interest to pay an electricity bill. Electricity costs 20 cent per unit. She used 250 units. The bill also has a standing charge of €30. Calculate the electricity bill.

(vii) Does Cathy have enough money from the interest to pay the electricity bill? Explain your answer.

Solution

(i) €8·65 × 40 = €346

(ii) Gross pay = 100% = €346

$$1\% = \frac{346}{100}$$

$$\text{Gross tax} = 20\% = \frac{346 \times 20}{100} = €69\cdot20.$$

(iii) Net tax = Gross tax − Tax credit
= €69·20 − €20 = €49·20

(iv) Amount Cathy is left with
= €346 − €49·20 = €296·80

(v) Principal = 100% = €1,650

$$1\% = \frac{1,650}{100}$$

$$\text{Interest} = 4\cdot5\% = \frac{1,650}{100} \times 4\cdot5 = €74\cdot25$$

This question was awarded a total of 31 marks. Part **(vi)** was awarded 10 of those marks. Do not get tired when answering such a long question. Your best concentration is required on every part of every question.

(vi) 250 units @ 20 cents each = 250 × 0·20 = €50
Standing charge = €30
Total bill = €80

(vii) Interest = €74·25 ⎫
Bill = €80 ⎬ Cathy is short (€80 − €74·25) by €5·75. She does not have enough money to pay the bill from the interest.